Sense in Translation

This innovative and interdisciplinary work brings together six essays which explore the complex relationship between linguistic translation and spatial translation and argue for an understanding of linguistic translation as an embodied phenomenon.

Integrating perspectives from philosophy, multilingual poetry and literature, as well as science and geometry, the book begins with a reading of translators Donald A. Landes' and Richard Howard's own notes on the translation and interpretation of the French words *sens* and *langue*. In the essays that follow, Rabourdin intertwines insights from both phenomenology and translation studies, engaging in notions of space, body, sense and language as filtered through a multilingual lens and drawing on a diversity of sources, including work from such figures as Jacques Derrida, Maurice Merleau-Ponty, Henri Poincaré, Michel Butor, Caroline Bergvall, Jean-Jacques Lecercle, Louis Wolfson and Lisa Robertson. This interdisciplinary thematic perspective highlights the need for an understanding of the experience of translation as neither distinctly linguistic nor spatial but one which fluidly allows for the bilingual body to sense and make sense.

This book offers a unique contribution to translation studies, comparative literature, French studies, and philosophy of language and will be of particular interest to students and scholars in these fields.

Caroline Rabourdin is an architect and writer. She is Senior Teaching Fellow in History and Theory and Architectural and Interdisciplinary Studies at the Bartlett School of Architecture at University College London, UK and teaches at the AA School of Architecture and at the University of Greenwich, London, UK.

Routledge Advances in Translation and Interpreting Studies

40 **Hybrid Englishes and the Challenges of/for Translation**
 Identity, Mobility and Language Change
 Edited by Karen Bennett and Rita Queiroz de Barros

41 **Translating the Visual**
 A Multimodal Perspective
 Rachel Weissbrod and Ayelet Kohn

42 **Using Computers in the Translation of Literary Style**
 Challenges and Opportunities
 Roy Youdale

43 **Concrete Poetry**
 Translation and Transmission
 Edited by John Corbett and Ting Huang

44 **Humour in Audiovisual Translation**
 Theories and Applications
 Margherita Dore

44 **Evaluating the Evaluator**
 A Novel Perspective on Translation Quality Assessment
 Hansjörg Bittner

45 **Sense in Translation**
 Essays on the Bilingual Body
 Caroline Rabourdin

For more information about this series, please visit https://www.routledge.com/Routledge-Advances-in-Translation-and-Interpreting-Studies/book-series/RTS

Sense in Translation
Essays on the Bilingual Body

Caroline Rabourdin

NEW YORK AND LONDON

First published 2020
by Routledge
52 Vanderbilt Avenue, New York, NY 10017

and by Routledge
2 Park Square, Milton Park, Abingdon, Oxon, OX14 4RN

Routledge is an imprint of the Taylor & Francis Group, an informa business

© 2020 Taylor & Francis

The right of Caroline Rabourdin to be identified as author of this work has been asserted by her in accordance with sections 77 and 78 of the Copyright, Designs and Patents Act 1988.

All rights reserved. No part of this book may be reprinted or reproduced or utilised in any form or by any electronic, mechanical, or other means, now known or hereafter invented, including photocopying and recording, or in any information storage or retrieval system, without permission in writing from the publishers.

Trademark notice: Product or corporate names may be trademarks or registered trademarks, and are used only for identification and explanation without intent to infringe.

Library of Congress Cataloging-in-Publication Data
A catalog record for this title has been requested

ISBN: 978-0-367-26699-8 (hbk)
ISBN: 978-0-429-29468-6 (ebk)

Typeset in Times New Roman
by codeMantra

Contents

Acknowledgements — vi

Introduction — 1

1 Translators' Notes: On Translating *'Sens'* and *'Langue'* in Merleau-Ponty's *Phénoménologie de la perception* and Ferdinand de Saussure's *Cours de linguistique générale* — 10

2 Sense in Translation: Geometrical Translation as an Embodied and Sensory Practice — 20

3 The Expanding Space of the Train Carriage: A Phenomenological Reading of Michel Butor's *La modification* — 36

4 Making Sense of Caroline Bergvall's Poetry: The Space between *les langues* and Lecercle's *Philosophy of Nonsense* — 55

5 Louis Wolfson's Reformed Body — 68

6 The Political Bilingual Body: One's Right to the Other Language — 81

Index — 93

Acknowledgements

Most chapters in this book originated as conference papers delivered in various countries and I am delighted that the collection of essays is now part of Routledge's Advances in Translation and Interpreting Studies series. My greatest thanks go to editor Elysse Preposi and the reviewers who recommended the book for the series.

I am also deeply grateful to the organisers, as well as anonymous reviewers of the conferences I have been invited to take part in. The conference calls were at the source of the essays developed in this volume, and to some extent also helped shape the research. In particular I would like to thank Johannes Riquet and Elizabeth Riquet for their interest in the work I presented at the Travelling Narratives conference (early on a Sunday morning!) and for their permission to reprint the essay "The Expanding Space of the Train Carriage: A Phenomenological Reading of Michel Butor's *La modification*" first published in *Spatial Modernities: Geographies Imagination, Narratives* (Routledge, 2018). The conference itself was a success and the experience marked a real turning point in my writing practice.

Many thanks to Alma Conway, editor of *CALL: Irish Journal for Culture, Arts, Literature and Language*, for allowing the use and re-working of parts of the essay "Spatial Translations and Embodied Bilingualism" in this volume, to Alain Berthoz for supplying a copy of his drawing of a running man (Figure 2.1) printed in Chapter 2, from his book *Le sens du mouvement* (Paris: Odile Jacob, 1997) and to Caroline Bergvall and Nightboat Books publishers for the permission to reprint parts of the poem "Crop" (*Meddle English*, New York: Nightboat Books, 2011).

The research has been facilitated by various institutions I have had the chance to teach and/or study at: I would like to thank University of the Arts London and the Student Research Fund, the AA School of Architecture and the Bartlett School of Architecture (UCL) Architecture Research Fund for supporting my participation to the conferences.

Acknowledgements

I would like to thank colleagues and friends, who, along the way, have read various drafts and made suggestions: Prof. Kristen Kreider for our discussions, her insightful suggestions and continuous encouragement, Claire Potter for the precision with which she read the manuscript, Ben Fitton for his recommendations on Jean-Jacques Lecercle, Prof. Peg Rawes for pointing at 'Sense' in the early stages of the research, Prof. Adrian Forty, who saw architectural qualities in the work, John O'Regan for his interest in the work and careful reading of the first draft.

My thanks also go to Bernice Donszelmann for her constant support, scrutiny and attentiveness throughout my research time at Chelsea College of Arts (UAL), as well as Ken Wilder and Brendan Prendeville for their valuable input. I would like to thank Dr. Maria Walsh and Prof. Tom Conley for their generosity in reviewing my PhD thesis – from which some of the essays originate – and for a memorable discussion which still resonates to this date.

Introduction

In his essay "Translation from Drawings to Buildings," architectural historian Robin Evans argues that the translation of words can be compared to the translation of geometrical figures from one point in space to another. Yet, the substratum across which they travel, he adds, is not isotropic and words get "bent, broken or lost on the way" (1997, 54). This description implies that words are autonomous objects of study, somehow disconnected from human experience, and also raises questions about the relationship between language and geometry. As an architect and bilingual writer, I contend that the relationship between linguistic translation and spatial translation is not reducible to simple analogy but instead offers a more complex and fertile relationship. I argue that linguistic translation and spatial translation relate at a fundamental level originating in the speaker's body. The premise of this collection of essays is therefore to consider language as an embodied and spatial practice, as has been developed by post-structuralist philosophers and by phenomenologists, and to consider linguistic translation as a lived phenomenon. Maurice Merleau-Ponty's conception of the body as expression and of the sensing body in particular is absolutely essential to this inquiry. By referring to Merleau-Ponty's work on *sens* and his analysis of relative and absolute movement, the aim is to develop an understanding of the corporeity of linguistic translation. Each of the following essays, with the exception of "Translators' Notes," originated as a conference paper, and each of them tackles the experience of translation, whether it be considered as linguistic or as spatial. Ultimately, what the essays endeavour to show is that these movements can no longer be categorised as distinct, but rather join in the capacity of our bodies to sense and in our desire to make sense.

There is something intrinsically spatial about the act of speaking or indeed writing. It involves the whole body. The movement asked for by the reader, or indeed the listener, is more than a simple rotation of the head, it involves a correlative translation of oneself into a different linguistic world, requiring a physical effort on the part of the reader/listener. The linguistic world, as described by Merleau-Ponty in *La phénoménologie de la perception*, is constituted through our personal experience of language and our successive encounters with words:

> [le langage] présente ou plutôt est la prise de position du sujet dans le monde de ses significations. Le terme de 'monde' n'est pas ici une manière de parler: il veut dire que la vie 'mentale' ou culturelle emprunte à la vie naturelle ses structures et que le sujet pensant doit être fondé sur le sujet incarné. Le geste phonétique réalise, pour le sujet parlant et pour ceux qui l'écoutent, une certaine structuration de l'expérience, une certaine modulation de l'existence, exactement comme un comportement de mon corps investit pour moi et pour autrui les objets qui m'entourent d'une certaine signification.
>
> (1945, 235)

> [language] presents, or rather it is, the subject's taking up of a position in the world of his significations. The term 'world' is here not just a manner of speaking: it means that 'mental' or cultural life borrows its structures from natural life and that the thinking subject must be grounded upon the embodied subject. For the speaking subject and for those who listen to him, the phonetic gesture produces a certain structuring of experience, a certain modulation of existence, just as a behavior of my body invests – for me and for others – the objects that surround me with a certain signification.
>
> (2012, 199)

As such, the speaking body's linguistic world is constituted incrementally, through a gradual process of sedimentation of the sensations words procure; the linguistic world is therefore subjective and in constant evolution, and depends on our bodily ability to make sense of each and every encounter with the words in various situations and various locations. Merleau-Ponty's lifelong work on expression and perception spans a range of disciplines: while his early work on "the body as expression" in *La phénoménologie de la perception* (1945) is based on scientific observations and clinical scrutiny, his later work, published posthumously as *La prose du monde* (1962), engages more directly with poetry and what he calls 'literary language.' Yet throughout his work, Merleau-Ponty's linguistic world appears to be essentially monolingual – and monocultural. He has surprisingly few words to say about bilingualism. However in the chapter "Le corps comme expression et la parole," where the notion of linguistic world is developed, Merleau-Ponty writes:

> Nous pouvons parler plusieurs langues, mais l'une d'elles reste toujours celle dans laquelle nous vivons. Pour assimiler complètement une langue, il faudrait assumer le monde qu'elle exprime et l'on appartient jamais à deux mondes à la fois.
> (1945, 228)

> We can speak several languages, but one of them always remains the one in which we live. In order to wholly assimilate a language, it would be necessary to take up the world it expresses, and we never belong to two worlds at the same time.
> (2012, 193)

Although isolated, this comment is rather startling. It is made all the more enigmatic by an accompanying quote by the writer T.E. Lawrence, included by Merleau-Ponty in a footnote, stating "madness was very near, as I believe it would be near the man who could see things through the veils at once of two customs, two educations, two environments" (Lawrence 1935, 30). Does Merleau-Ponty imply with his assertion and the reference to T.E. Lawrence that any attempt to be 'fully' bilingual would necessarily lead the speaker to madness [*folie*]? To assume that one cannot live in another language would be a denial of any constituted bodily sense the 'other' language produces and would problematise the very possibility of the bilingual subject. I would like to think instead that Merleau-Ponty's argument hinges on the words 'simultaneously,' and 'at the same time': one may indeed live in several linguistic worlds, but at different times, at intervals. Inhabiting one language after another, travelling across and between languages, making the movement across languages part of language itself is understood here through Merleau-Ponty's writings on mobility where the speaking body makes the effort, the muscular effort even, to move towards one or the other language.

The essays in this volume belong to the tradition of the literary essay, indebted to Michel de Montaigne and later developed by Jacques Derrida and Hélène Cixous, where 'Essay' comes from Old

French *'essai,'* and the verb *'essaier'* (later *'essayer'*), which means 'to try' or 'test.' The essay is an attempt and a trial and therefore is not concerned with totality or completeness. To write an *essay*, is *to say* and many of the works by other authors I refer to and engage with in the following essays originated as verbal addresses and performances. Cixous' *Three Steps on the Ladder of Writing* (1993) was delivered as a series of lectures, Caroline Bergvall's poetry was performed to an audience and the reader will remember also that Ferdinand de Saussure did not write the *Cours de linguistique générale* (1916) in their published form. What is commonly referred to as *The Cours* has in fact been compiled from various lecture notes that Saussure's students found in his desk in combination with transcripts they had themselves written while sitting on university benches. One should therefore avoid the phrase "Saussure writes," in favour of "Saussure says," which in its longer version would read "Saussure's students write that Saussure says." Notes such as the following one about Cixous' "Difficult Joys" typically accompany the publication of conference papers and lectures' transcriptions:

> When originally given, this paper was developed from bare notes written in French; the process of speaking it involved expansion and translation simultaneously. We hope that this printed version can still reflect the improvisatory freshness of the original.
> (1990, 5)

The 'improvisatory freshness' referred to here corresponds to what Merleau-Ponty names *le langage parlant* (1962, 17): language that creates itself at the time of utterance and invites the listener to make sense in the moment. In her preface to Book XI of Michel Butor's *Œuvres complètes,* entirely dedicated to what the author calls his *Improvisations,* Mireille Calle-Gruber (2010) describes the texts as a transcription of his *parole vive*. Butor's *Improvisations* began as lectures in various universities; he delivered these lectures without the recourse to any notes, with only bookmarks amongst the pages of the books he was referring to. Each lecture was for Butor a *'nouveau voyage.'* These lectures were recorded, then transcribed and finally re-written with particular attention to *keeping the parole alive*. The essays in this volume, however, have not been improvised. Unlike Butor's *Improvisations*, the words have materialised through the pen or the keyboard first. I would not, could not, *say* what I write. Each essay collected in this volume was initiated by a conference call and was written 'in order to be read,' as such the international conference became both the motivation and the space where the research was deployed, where it was made possible. Academic conferences and international symposia have been the site of the research and the presentation of papers offered scope for development and testing. In "Signature, événement, context" (1972), Derrida writes – or rather talks[1] – about the *communication*, the French translation of the 'conference paper.' He challenges the assumption that the speaker might be required to convey meaning in their *communication*; he also points at the absence of the recipient at the time of writing the *communication*, and, later, at the absence of the writer in the printed version of the paper. The 'physical absence' of the audience at the time of writing, which Derrida describes in his *communication*, is replaced, he adds, by the 'intentional presence' of the audience, albeit in the distance. And so, in writing the essays, I addressed successively various audiences of linguists, artists, geographers or writers, and the essays in this volume are as diverse as the conference calls they were responding to.

The first chapter is the only exception to the rule, as it was not prepared for a conference. It should be read as preparatory work to the rest of the book and serve as an expanded glossary of the words *'sens'* and *'langue'* which I refer to throughout the book. The research engages with Merleau-Ponty's *sens* and Saussure's *langues*, but the chapter, instead of turning to the source texts, pays particular attention to the way that translators have understood and translated the words into English. A close reading of Roy Harris and Donald A. Landes' respective introductions to Ferdinand de Saussure's *Course in General Linguistics* (1983) and Merleau-Ponty's *Phenomenology of Perception* (2012) shows, for instance, how Colin's Smith translation of the word *sens* (Merleau-Ponty, 1962) has led Landes to undertake a retranslation of Merleau-Ponty's masterpiece. Other translators' introductions are referred to, such as Peggy Kamuf's translator's note to Jacques Derrida's *The Ear of the Other* (1985), stressing not only the problems but also the new possibilities offered by such multilingual and comparative readings.

The second chapter is the synthesis of two separate essays: one was written for the "Translation: Exchange of Ideas" conference organised by the University of Cardiff in Wales, while the other essay was initially presented at the International Language Symposium in Dublin on the theme "Language, Migration, Diaspora." Both conferences were organised by Modern Languages University Departments, yet for these presentations I approached translation on a purely geometrical level. In this chapter I address Robin Evan's analogy between linguistic and geometrical translation by turning to geometry, and the philosophy of geometry in particular with the work of Henri Poincaré and Edmund Husserl on translation. French mathematician and philosopher of science, Poincaré (1902), explains how the physical body is intrinsically related to our understanding of geometry and absolute movement and establishes that translation can only be understood through a correlative movement of the body. Like Husserl in *"The Origin of Geometry"* ([1939] 1989), he acknowledges the primacy of bodily experience in understanding geometrical translation. In an attempt to test Evans' analogy between geometrical and linguistic translation, the chapter maps out the various possible linguistic transformations and transpositions of the word 'umbrella' according to Saussure's principle of differentiation (1916), thereby highlighting the geometrical transformations of the word across different linguistic worlds. What the chapter aims to show is that the linguistic transformations of the word 'umbrella' are accompanied by what Husserl refers to as an originary and bodily *sense* of translation.

The third chapter was first delivered in Zurich at the "Travelling Narratives: Modernity and the Spatial Imaginary" Conference at the English Department of the University of Zurich and later published in the *Spatial Modernities: Geography, Narratives, Imaginaries* volume edited by Johannes Riquet and Elizabeth Kollmann (2018). The conference took place in English, but Zurich, like Cardiff and Dublin where previous chapters were delivered, is no stranger to the multilingual debate. This chapter concentrates on the work of French author Michel Butor. While Butor's work is varied and proteiform, ranging from poetry to critical essays, for this chapter, I undertake a phenomenological reading of Butor's novel *La modification* (1957), a fiction based on the train journey of the main character between Paris and Rome. The narrative itself is articulated entirely by the main character around the movement of a train and memories from the past as well as projections into the future taking place in one or another city. There is an obvious sense of directionality throughout the novel, and Butor's treatment of movement owes much to phenomenology. Through concomitant readings of Butor's novel, his critical essay about the space of the novel *L'espace du roman* (1964) and Merleau-Ponty's *Phénoménologie de la perception* (1945), the chapter shows how the body of the reader is placed by Butor at the centre of the reading experience. It shows that the linguistic movement of the reader, like Merleau-Ponty's *geste*, is intentional and requires an *effort* on the part of the reader.

The fourth chapter, originally delivered as a paper in Reykjavik for the "Art in Translation" conference organised by the University of Iceland, directly addresses bilingual experiences through the work of multilingual artist and poet Caroline Bergvall. If in previous chapters, I had been referring to works written either in French or in English, Bergvall's piece is the first to be written in French *and* English, as well as in Norwegian, a language I do not understand. This situation brings to the fore the notion of 'non-sense' which I define here in relation to, and differing from, Jean-Jacques Lecercle's philosophy of 'nonsense' (1994). Both Bergvall and Lecercle write about the violence of language. In this chapter, I proceed to an interpretation of Bergvall's poem "Crop" (2011), showing at first what might appear as a series of translations, but instead operates as a series of slippages and breaks between one language and the next. In her poem, Bergvall questions the body's integrity between languages: if the body is cropped and truncated during its travels across languages, as Bergvall suggests, its integrity is only retained if considered across the range of languages it uses.

The fifth chapter engages with what may to a certain extent be considered as a literary piece of self-translation. *Le Schizo et les langues ou La Phonétique chez le psychotique: Esquisses d'un étudiant de langues schizophrénique* (1970) by the American author Louis Wolfson was seen, at the time of publication, and still is, unclassifiable.[2] Wolfson could not bear the English language and instead chose to write in French, a language he learnt in textbooks and dictionaries. I first presented the essay from which the chapter stems in 2016 at the ACLA Annual conference held at Harvard University, as part of the "Writing between worlds: Multilingualism as a Creative Force" panel. The essay attempts to show how multilingualism is for Wolfson a *necessary* force. It shows how Wolfson's use of language is the absolute translation of a distressed body, desperately attempting to *make sense* again in a newly found language. Wolfson's autobiographical book is the writing of the self in a foreign language, and yet the piece itself is intrinsically untranslatable. More surprisingly perhaps, it also shows how *folie*, the absence of sense and a return to a pre-linguistic state, can be integral part of the multilingual experience, and by extension, any work of translation.

The final chapter, written some time later, looks more specifically at the condition of the nomadic speaker and considers the relationship of the speaking body to the 'other' language. The other language here is understood as the second language, learnt in the host country of the nomadic speaker. Starting from Lisa Robertson's definition of 'prosody of citizenship' (2018), this chapter uses Derrida's remarks on absolute and conditional hospitality in order to define the linguistic subjectivity of the speaking subject in relation to the laws that govern it. Following the 2016 Brexit vote in the UK, the rights of millions of Europeans living in the UK are under threat and the chapter looks at how their linguistic subjectivity might be altered as a result. This essay, first presented at the 23rd International Symposium for Phenomenology organised by Emmanuel Alloa, Delia Popa and Shela Sheikh in Perugia, Italy, was written in French and translated into English for this book. The English version should therefore be read as the author's first piece of self-translation, and the reader will most certainly detect the unease that the translation has caused. This final chapter is not a conclusion, but rather the beginning of a new line of inquiry in which the sensing body is included in the definition and mapping of bilingual, and possibly also multilingual, subjectivities.

This book does not aim towards any sense of completion, but it is the author's hope that the writing experience may lead to and encounter many more discussions, on the sense of movement that the bilingual body experiences in perpetual translation.

Notes

1 "Signature, événement, contexte" was first presented as a *communication* at the Congrès International des Sociétés de Philosophie de langue française in Montréal, in August 1971. The theme of the symposium was "La communication."
2 See *Dossier Wolfson, ou, L'affaire du Schizo et les langues* (2009) for details of the controversy about the publication of his first book by Gallimard in the *Connaissance de l'inconscient* collection.

Works Cited

Bergvall, Caroline. 2011. "Crop" in *Meddle English*. New York: Night Boat Books.
Butor, Michel. 1957. *La modification.* Paris: Les Editions de Minuit.
———. 1964. *L'espace du roman.* Paris: Les Editions de Minuit.
Calle-Gruber, Mireille. 2010. Preface to *Œuvres completes*, *Improvisations*, volume 11, by Michel Butor, edited by Mireille Calle-Gruber. Paris: Editions de la Différence.
Cixous, Hélène. 1993. *Three Steps on the Ladder of Writing.* New York: Columbia University Press.
Cixous, Hélène. 1990. "Difficult Joys" in *The Body and the Text: Hélène Cixous, Reading and Teaching*, edited by Helen Wilcox, Keith McWatters,

Ann Thomson and Linda R. Williams. Hemel Hempstead: Harvester Wheatsheaf.
Derrida, Jacques. 1972. "Signature, événement, contexte" in *Marges de la philosophie*. Paris: Editions de Minuit.
———. 1997. *De l'Hospitalité / Anne Dufourmantelle invite Jacques Derrida à répondre*. Paris: Calmann-Lévy.
Evans, Robin. 1997. *Translations from Drawing to Building and Other Essays*. London: Janet Evans and Architectural Association Publications.
Husserl, Edmund. [1939] 1962. *L'Origine de la géométrie*, translated by Jacques Derrida. Paris: Presses Universitaires de France.
———. [1939] 1989. "The Origin of Geometry", translated by David Carr in *Edmund Husserl's 'Origin of Geometry': and Introduction / Jacques Derrida*, with a Preface and Afterword by John P. Leavy Jr. Lincoln: University of Nebraska Press.
Kamuf, Peggy. 1985. Translator's Introduction to *The Ear of the Other: Otobiography, Transference, Translation*, edited by Claude Lévesque and Christie McDonald. New York: Schocken Books.
Lawrence, T.E. 1935. *The Seven Pillars of Wisdom*. London: Jonathan Cape.
Lecercle, Jean-Jacques. 1994. *Philosophy of Nonsense*. London: Routledge.
Merleau-Ponty, Maurice. 1945. *Phénoménologie de la perception*. Paris: Gallimard.
———. 1962. *Phenomenology of Perception*, translated by Colin Smith. London: Routledge.
———. 2012. *Phenomenology of Perception*, translated by Donald A. Landes. Oxon: Routledge.
Poincaré, Henri. [1902] 1968. *La Science et l'Hypothèse*. Paris: Flammarion.
Pontalis, Jean-Bertrand, Jean-Marie Gustave Le Clézio, Paul Auster, Piera Aulagnier, Max Dorra, Michel Foucault, Pierre Alferi and François Cusset. 2009. *Dossier Wolfson, ou, L'affaire du Schizo et les langues*. Paris: Gallimard.
Rabourdin, Caroline. 2018. "The Space of the Expanding Carriage: Phenomenological Reading of Michel Butor's *La modification*" in *Spatial Modernities: Geography, Narratives, Imaginaries*, edited by Elizabeth Kollman and Johannes Riquet. London: Routledge.
Robertson, Lisa. 2018. *Thresholds: A Prosody of Citizenship*. London: Book Works and The Common Guild.
Saussure, Ferdinand de. 1916. *Cours de linguistique générale*. Paris: Edtions Payot & Rivages.
———. 1983. *Course in General Linguistics*, translated by Roy Harris. London: Gerald Duckworth & Co.
Wolfson, Louis. 1970. *Le Schizo et les langues ou La phonétique chez le psychotique: Esquisses d'un étudiant de langues schizophrénique*. Paris: Gallimard.

1 Translators' Notes
On Translating '*Sens*' and '*Langue*' in Merleau-Ponty's *Phénoménologie de la perception* and Ferdinand de Saussure's *Cours de linguistique générale*

During the course of my research I have read many introductions to translated texts only to discover self-justified attempts at clarification, contextualisation and processes of disambiguation; and in some cases, what the translated text loses is precisely this precious ambiguity. The desire for clarification, motivated by the illusion of a language where meaning would be universal and fixed, destroys thought's complexity. It forbids connections, fluidity, movement. It works against language, not with language. I wish simply to note here the difficulties that others have encountered in translating some key terms often referred to in the following essays from French to English.

One of the most striking examples of the destructive need for disambiguation can be found in the English translation of Saussure's *Cours de linguistique générale* (1916), where ironically, the key word, the fundamental word even of Saussure's theory, is subjected to such reduction. In his preface to *Course in General Linguistics* (1983), published some 70 years after the publication of the original French text, translator Roy Harris makes the distinction between *langue* and *langage*, which seems appropriate given the importance of the distinction in Saussure's theory:

> On crossing the Channel Saussure has been made to utter such blatantly unSaussurean pronouncements as 'language is a form, not a substance'. Surprisingly few have seen that it is not at all necessary to make heavy weather of the distinction between *langage* and *langue* provided one respects the important semantic difference in English between using the word *language* with and without an article.
>
> (1983, xiii–xiv)

But a couple of pages later he writes the rather perplexing lines:

> Finally, some of the central problems of interpretation of the *Cours de linguistique générale* hinge on the fact that the word *langue* seems to be used in a variety of ways. [...] The result is that even the technical uses of the term *langue* sometimes seem to be at odds with one another. To what extent this is due to unwitting vacillation on the part of Saussure or his editors is a matter for debate.
>
> (1983, xv–xvi)

Harris goes on to identify two possible solutions to what he describes as the problem: the first solution would be "to fix upon a single all-purpose translation of the word *langue* and stick to it throughout, leaving the reader to cope with the complexities of interpretation for himself" and the second solution, adopted in his translation, is "to indicate the full range of implications associated with the term *langue* by using different renderings in different contexts." And so the English translation is dotted with expressions such as 'linguistic structure' and 'linguistic system,' where the original simply uses the word *langue*, all in the name of clarity. Finally he admits:

> Varying the translation of a key theoretical term may perhaps be objected to in principle on grounds of inconsistency. But the inconsistency in this case is superficial; whereas in compensation one gains the possibility of expressing nuances and emphases in Saussure's thought which would otherwise risk being lost to the English reader.
>
> (1983, xv–xvi)

In doing so, Roy Harris has explicitly stripped the *Cours* of one of its crucial nuances. That the distinction between *langage/langue*, rendered with the distinction language/a language, be subtle and easily missed is obvious and unquestionable, but what the English reader loses here is the connection, or more precisely the connotation, between *langue* and *langage* in French. What the reader is given with translations such as *linguistic structure* and *linguistic system* is an interpretation that does not give the reader the chance to choose – actively – between one and the other meaning. The reader loses the right to make sense of the text themselves.

The proximity of the words *langue* and *langage* in French asks the reader to oscillate between meanings; what Harris calls an 'unwitting oscillation' cannot reasonably be unwitting since, as I believe, the experience or act of oscillation itself should remain part of the text. The astonishing thing here is the admission by the translator himself that his interpretations have replaced *langue* for the sake of simplification, in order to alleviate or even eradicate difficulty in the text.

In his translation of Roland Barthes' *Image, Music, Text*, Stephen Heath (1977) encounters the same problem, but deals with it slightly differently. In the Translator's Notes, he explains a series of difficulties he has come across during the translation:

> *Langue/parole* – The reference here is to the distinction made by the Swiss linguist Saussure. Where *parole* is the realm of the individual moments of language use, of particular 'utterances' or 'messages', whether spoken or written, *langue* is the system or code ('*le code de la langue*') which allows the realization of the individual messages. As the language-system, object of linguistics, *langue* is thus also to be differentiated from language, the heterogeneous totality with which the linguist is initially faced and which may be studied from a variety of points of view, partaking as it does to the physical, the psychological, the mental, the individual and the social. It is precisely by delimiting its specific object and fixing as its task the description of that object (that is, of the *langue*, the system of the language) that Saussure founds linguistics as a science. [...] The problem in translation is that in English 'language' has to serve both *langue* and *langage*. *Langue* can often be specified by translation as 'a' or 'the language' or again as 'language-system' (in opposition to the 'language-use' of *parole*), but I have included the French term in brackets in cases where the idea of the analytic construction of a language-system is being given crucial stress [...].
>
> (1977, 7–8)

As well as serving as a useful reminder of Saussure's concepts and terminology, Heath explains how he dealt with the tandem *langue/langage*, which like Roy Harris, he describes as a 'problem' to be solved. Heath has chosen to introduce the article 'a' or 'the' before language as a way of distinguishing *langue* from *langage*, just as Roy Harris suggested but eventually rejected. He also chose to retain the original French word into the text, whether it be *langue* or *langage*, in a more direct and slightly intrusive way – but one widely accepted in translation practice – with the use of square brackets. Brackets, footnotes, endnotes, are the only tropes of the 'visible' translator. Here, the translator is at work, and the invisible process of translation is made visible. The space of footnotes, pages of introductory notes and prefaces are spaces in the translated book where the translator is explicitly visible, and the only space where s/he is not subordinate to the author of the text s/he is working with. It is a space of his/her own, even if still about the translation. Translator Brice Matthieussent goes as far as making the footnotes central to the text in his book *Vengeance du traducteur* (2009), where extended footnotes take the place of the translated text.

Looking back at Harris' and Heath's notes, however, one can't help but notice how they both fail to mention that *langue* is also part of the body in the French language, a body part: the tongue. This observation, of course, would not be helpful or necessary to their intended process of disambiguation. It is worth noting nonetheless since it adds to the ambiguity in the French version, an ambiguity, polysemy, which does not translate into English. And so this dimension of the *langue* is lost to the English reader. *Langue*, contrarily to what Harris or even Heath might think, is not only a 'language-system or code,' but also, and I would say primarily, a part of the body. Any child learning French at an early age would learn the word *'langue'* alongside other body parts such as *'œil,' 'nez,' 'oreille'* or *'bouche'* ['eye,' 'nose,' 'ear' or 'mouth'], blissfully unaware that the word *langue* is also the 'language-system' or code she/he is learning when saying those words. And so the *langue* is one of the instruments of *langue*. The role of the tongue is discussed in great detail in Saussure's *Cours de linguistique générale.* In the chapter dedicated to phonology, one can read a quasi-medical description of the *cavité buccale*, indicating how certain movements of the tongue contribute to the making of specific sounds. The description is purely mechanical. It is fair to note that Saussure is not usually remembered for his lectures on anatomy, and the editors admit to having added to Saussure's original lectures.[1] In a note (Saussure 1919, 66), they explain that Saussure's original description was rather succinct and that they found it necessary to supplement it with information from Otto Jespersen's *Lehrbuch der Phonetik* (1904). The extensive technical description of the vocal apparatus in the *Cours* is accompanied by the following graphic illustration.

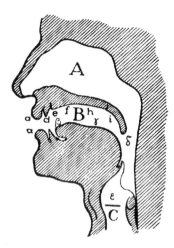

Figure 1.1 Diagram in Ferdinand de Saussure's *Cours de linguistique générale* (Paris: Payot 1916, 67).

Whether Saussure had intended it or not, the *Cours* have ultimately severed the tongue/mouth and nasal cavity from the rest of the body. Isolating the tongue, cleft and teeth certainly helps in decomposing their respective movements but the separation appears somewhat arbitrary. The lungs, although mentioned in the description, are not shown in the illustration. The head stands alone, disconnected from the rest of the body and it is worth noting that this depiction stands in clear contrast to Maurice Merleau-Ponty's description of the body as expression involving the entire body in *Phénoménologie de la perception* (1945).

Saussure's ambition, as we know, is to establish linguistics as a science, built empirically and *objectively*. And we know also of Merleau-Ponty's claim that "Phenomenology's most important accomplishment is [...] to have joined an extreme subjectivism with an extreme objectivism" (Merleau-Ponty 1945, 20). For his research Merleau-Ponty himself draws from a variety of disciplines, whether scientific or literary for instance. In the introduction to *Phénoménologie de la perception*, he sets out to redefine *sensation*, which he qualifies as the most confused notion there is. Yet he adds that *sensation* is also the most fundamental to the understanding of the phenomenon of perception. Here, he lays the foundations of phenomenology on an ambiguity, on moving grounds, defying any accepted definition of the notion of sensation. He undertakes his description of sensation by describing the notion *in relation* to science and philosophy, thus putting an end to the traditional opposition between the lines of thought. This way, instead of emerging in the lineage of one discipline or in opposition to the other, phenomenology creates a new space between these disciplines and emerges in a truly relational situation. If sensation has different interpretations and developments in physiology, biology and psychology, Merleau-Ponty embraces them all.

We understand then, that the word '*sens*' may have perplexed many a translator attempting to translate Merleau-Ponty's *Phénoménologie de la perception*. Donald Landes admitted to having decided to undertake a new translation because of his frustration at the handling of the word in Colin Smith's existing translation. For Landes, Smith simply fails to acknowledge the polysemy of the word *sens*, as he writes in the Introduction:

> One of the first motivations for a new translation was the previous translator's non-systematic treatment of Merleau-Ponty's use of *sens* and *signification*. Sens is a difficult term to translate, as it means 'meaning', 'sense' and 'direction'. Wherever the context has allowed I have translated it as 'sense', which in English preserves the richness of the French term, while reserving 'meaning' for Merleau-Ponty's occasional use of the construction *vouloir dire* (to 'mean' or, literally, to 'want to say').
>
> (2012, xlviii)

Whereas we might disagree with the translation of *vouloir dire* into *meaning*, because it lacks the notion of intentionality which Merleau-Ponty insists on, the persistence [insistence] on the use of 'sense' however has definitely improved the translation and the text indeed reads better than the previous translation, to the French reader at least. Implied in this polysemy is the fact that 'meaning,' 'sense' and 'direction' cannot be studied independently of one another in our search for sense, but must be seen in relation to one another and can only exist with one another. The words relate to each other *in movement*, in our oscillation between the three possible significations when we talk about sense.

Reading Alain Berthoz' book title *Le sens du mouvement* (1997) for instance, without prior knowledge of Berthoz' work, one might legitimately ask whether the book is about the direction of movement, its *sensing* or even, and why not, the *meaning* of movement. The fact is that, although written by a physiologist and at times very technical, the book is not only about the perception and physiological enactment of movement but also about the philosophy of movement, and Berthoz' title reflects the all-encompassing quality of his research. Unfortunately the English translation of the book has received the familiar *disambiguation* treatment we have seen above and Berthoz's title became *The Brain's Sense of Movement* (2000) in its English version. If the English title strives for clarification, it also leaves out an important idea of the book, namely that movement is not perceived solely in the brain, but that it is a sensation perceived with and through the whole body. If the reader identifies Berthoz's translated book as a purely neurological study, something has been lost from the overriding meaning and intention of the author that underlines the relational aspect of the perception of movement. The translator here has decapitated the sensing body and only kept the brain.

In this volume, whenever possible, ambiguity and polysemy have been retained and sometimes encouraged as part of the methodology.

Saussure in his *Cours* explains that terms "are not defined positively by their content, but rather negatively by their relationships with the other terms of the system. Their most exact characteristic is to be what the others are not" (Saussure 1916, 162 trans. my own). I will leave aside the negative terminology to concentrate on the principle of differentiation. Saussure insists on both the arbitrary and differential qualities of words.[2] Interestingly, Saussure himself uses the example of an interlingual translation in order to illustrate the principle of differentiation happening within the same language: he explains that *mouton* translates into either *sheep* or *mutton* and therefore does not have the same value as either of them independently, since it refers to both of them. *Mouton* is not *mutton* is not *sheep*. Translators are not only aware of these differences, they dwell in those differences.

Saussure tells us that differentiation is the basis of all languages and the notion has been further tested by Jacques Derrida (1972) in his famous essay titled "La différance," where the principle of differentiation not only takes a temporal quality but is also tested against both spoken and written language. Here, I will quote Peggy Kamuf's introductory note to her translation of *L'Oreille de l'autre: otobiographies, transferts, traductions: textes et débats avec Jacques Derrida*. She undertakes the difficult task of explaining Derrida's "La différance" to the English reader:

> Derrida forges this word at the intersection of the spatial and the temporal senses of the verb *différer*: to differ and to defer. The standard spelling of the noun *différence* corresponds only

to the first, spatial sense; there is no standard noun formed from the second sense of temporal deferral. The -ance ending conforms to the orthographics of a middle voice: neither active, nor passive, both active and passive (as in resonance). With the term, Derrida designates the movement of differentiation and deferral, spacing and temporalization which must be thought of as preceding and comprehending any propositioning of identifiable differences or oppositions. Significantly for Derrida's deconstruction of the traditional, philosophical opposition of speech and writing, the difference between *différence* and *différance* is unpronounced.

(1985, xi)

With *différance,* Derrida challenges Saussure's claim of the supremacy of spoken language over written language. *La différance,* was initially delivered as a lecture – and here I carefully choose the word lecture over paper – at the Société Française de Philosophie in 1968. It was a verbal address in which the 'a' of *différance* is not heard and remains silent, whereas the written paper, published the same year, visually shows and depicts difference. The relation between spoken language and written language are explored further in some of the essays of this volume, which also originated as verbal addresses.

L'Oreille de l'autre (1982) is the publication of seminars and round tables on the themes of autobiography and translation, which took place at the Université de Montréal in 1979 and therefore also originated as spoken word and parole. The title translates into the English publication as *The Ear of the Other.* Contrary to the translation of Berthoz' title, the English version of the book title does not edit down, but rather expands on possible meanings. The translated title imparts additional meanings that the original did not convey: thus, the 'ear' is not only the *oreille,* the organ, but also, to the bilingual reader attempting to make sense of the English title, the noun connotes the verb 'hear.' This new association establishes a *rapport à l'autre* through the action of hearing. It introduces the idea of the receiver, which *l'oreille* doesn't necessarily imply, for it is a noun, and might simply refer to a body part, its morphology, or constitution. *To hear* introduces an action, an active participation. The ear in *The Ear of the Other* also connotes the word 'here' as in 'the here of the other,' introducing a spatial and situated quality that the French title doesn't have. So the English title here, better than the French, encapsulates in five words some of Derrida's fundamental principles.

Architectural historian Adrian Forty in his book *Words and Buildings: A Vocabulary of Modern Architecture* (2000) is particularly aware of the non-equivalence of key architectural words across different languages and gives both a historical and geographical account of their differences within the chapters of his book. For example, in a chapter devoted to Space, he explains the difference between the German *Raum*, the French *Espace* and the English *Space*. However, rather than seeing differences as problematic, he insists on these differences in a very constructive and positive manner:

> Although the trade between languages is in some respects a difficulty in a book like this, in another sense the problem of translation is simply a manifestation of the transitoriness of meaning that is central to the whole enquiry: the migration of ideas and words from one language to another is another aspect of what goes on within a single language as one metaphor is displaced by another. Because this book is written in English, the terms with which it deals are terms as they exist in the English language. Quotations from other languages have been translated into English, which, although this contradicts the very point that words mean particular things within the language they are spoken, and tends towards the impression of a universal language of architecture, seemed necessary to make the book at all readable. But we should not regard the act of translation, as it often is regarded, as 'a problem', for through translation words gain as well as lose.
>
> (2000, 16)

Forty writes as an historian; he traces the meanings of words back to the cultures they originated from; as a philologist he establishes lineages and comparisons between various terminologies and understands all the nuances gained in the transit of words across languages. The essays in this volume draw from this comparative approach and attempt to show how the rich and accumulative layering of meanings acquired in translation is experienced through the movement of the sensing body. The essays will almost refer constantly to two languages: the words 'sense' and 'translation' in *Sense in Translation* will be understood in both the English language and the French language. I will therefore ask the reader to consider the concepts not in the single language I have chosen to write the essays in, but in both the English and French languages in which they stand.

Notes

1 As explained in the introduction, Saussure's *Cours* were not published by Saussure himself, but published after his death by Charles Bailly and Albert Séchehaye with the collaboration of Albert Riedlinger, from Saussure's notes and transcripts of students attending his lectures.
2 I use 'words' here to cover both the signified/signifier, which might also be called a linguistic entity.

Works Cited

Berthoz, Alain. 1997. *Le sens du movement.* Paris: Odile Jacob.
———. 2000. *The Brain's Sense of Movement*, translated by Giselle Weiss. Cambridge: Harvard University Press.
Derrida, Jacques. 1972. "La différance" in *Marges de la Philosophie.* Paris: Editions de Minuit.
Forty, Adrian. 2000. *Words and Buildings: A Vocabulary of Modern Architecture.* London: Thames & Hudson.
Harris, Roy. 1983. Translator's Introduction to *Course in General Linguistics, by Ferdinand de Saussure.* London: Gerald Duckworth & Co.
Heath, Stephen. 1977. Translator's Note in *Image, Music, Text*, by Roland Barthes. London: Fontana Press.
Jespersen, Otto. 1904. *Lehrbuch der Phonetik.* Leipzig: B. G. Teubner
Kamuf, Peggy. 1985. Translator's Introduction to *The Ear of the Other: Otobiography, Transference, Translation*, edited by Claude Lévesque and Christie McDonald. New York: Schocken Books.
Landes, Donald A. 2012. Translator's Introduction to *Phenomenology of Perception*, by Maurice Merleau-Ponty. Oxon: Routledge.
Lévesque, Claude and Christie McDonald, ed. 1982. *L'Oreille de l'autre: otobiographies, transferts, traduction: textes et débats avec Jacques Derrida.* Montreal: Vlb.
Matthieussent, Brice. 2009. *Vengeance du traducteur.* Paris: P.O.L.

2 Sense in Translation
Geometrical Translation as an Embodied and Sensory Practice[1]

In French, the word *translation*, although used in geometry and physics, is not used in linguistics anymore and has given way to the word *traduction* from Latin *traducere*, which means to "lead across, from one point to another." The word *traducere* was introduced by Italian writer L.A. Bruni around 1400 and widely used in the second half of the fifteenth century and *traduire* has now completely replaced the verb *translater*.[2] The primary meaning of the French word *translation* is to move from one place to another. From a scientific and architectural standpoint, I associate the word *translation* with vectors and spatial transformations. '*Translation,*' for me, is thus not a linguistic transformation; '*translation*' is primarily a geometrical transformation. In Euclidean geometry, a translation will simply move points from a point A to a point B without any distortion, in isotropic space.

In 1986, British architect and theoretician Robin Evans starts his famous essay "Translation from Drawing to Building" with the following analogy:

> To translate is to convey. It is to move something without altering it. This is its original meaning and this is what happens in translatory motion. Such too, by analogy with translatory motion, the translation of languages. Yet the substratum across which the sense of words is translated from language to language does not appear to have the requisite evenness and continuity; things can get bent, broken or lost on the way. The assumption that there is uniform space through which meaning may glide without modulation is more than just a naïve delusion, however. Only by assuming its pure and unconditional existence in the first place can any precise knowledge of the pattern of deviations from this imaginary condition be gained.
>
> (1997, 154)

Unfortunately Evans doesn't expand on the pattern of deviations from the ideal condition of spatial translation in his essay, nor does he develop the analogy between spatial translation and linguistic translation any further. Instead, his example is concerned with the translation from drawings to buildings, which is a complex subject, and uses the no less complex subject of translation from one language to the other only as a way of introduction. Here, I will look at the pure and ideal translatory motion as described by Evans and show that geometrical translation is not only a construct born out of arbitrary conventions, but also a sensory construct. As a French-speaking architect, my research seeks to understand the *bilingual phenomenon* by bringing together theories and practices about Space, Language and the Body as well as ultimately develop a notion of *Embodied Bilingualism*.

To embark on this geometrical journey, I would like to turn, or perhaps return, to the simplicity of Euclidian space. To consider Euclidian space today with its three idealised dimensions might sound reductive and somehow outmoded, but I believe that understanding the basic principles of geometrical translation might help us understand the phenomenon of linguistic translation as described by Evans. The OED simply describes Euclidean as "Relating to or denoting the system of geometry based on the work of Euclid and corresponding to the geometry of ordinary experience" (*Oxford English Dictionary*, 2nd ed., s.v. "Euclidean"). The words, 'Ordinary experience' remain evasive but Euclidian space, according to this definition, would therefore relate to our ordinary experience in and of the world.

At the turn of the 20th century, Henri Poincaré, eminent French mathematician, physicist and engineer, significantly contributed to the philosophy of science and shed light on the relationship between geometry and ordinary experience. In *Science and Hypothesis* (1902), he explains that, "One geometry cannot be more true than another; it can only be more convenient. Now, Euclidean geometry is, and will remain, the most convenient" ([1905] (1952), 59). He gives two reasons for his assertion: first because it is the simplest geometry and second, because it agrees with the properties of natural solids, which we can compare and measure by means of our senses. The essential Euclidean properties are that space

– is continuous,
– is infinite,
– has three dimensions,

– is homogeneous; that is, all its points are identical to one another,
– is isotropic, that is, that all straight lines (or *droites* in French) going through the same point are identical to one another.

Poincaré acknowledges that other types of geometry would be just as valid and illustrates by giving the following example:

> Imaginons un monde uniquement peuplé d'êtres dénués d'épaisseur; et supposons que ces animaux "infiniment plats" soient tous dans le même plan et n'en puissent sortir. Admettons de plus que ce monde soit assez éloigné des autres pour être soustrait à leur influence. Pendant que nous sommes en train de faire des hypothèses, il ne nous en coûte pas plus de douer ces êtres de raisonnement et de les croire capables de faire de la géométrie. Dans ce cas, ils n'attribueront certainement à l'espace que deux dimensions.
> ([1902] 1968, 65)

> Imagine a world uniquely peopled by beings of no thickness; and suppose these 'infinitely flat' animals are all in the same plane and cannot get out. Admit besides that this world is sufficiently far from others to be free from their influence. While we are making hypotheses, it costs us no more to endow these beings with reason and believe them capable of creating a geometry. In that case, they will certainly attribute to space only two dimensions.
> ([1902] 1913, 57)

For Poincaré, geometry is all about conventions, but those conventions that we use are not entirely arbitrary and owe their characteristics to our very own body constitution. They exist because of how we are in the world.

Poincaré's theoretical view of 1902 is reinforced today by physiological studies and the advanced scientific understanding of the body's constitution; demonstration of this is made, for instance, in *Le Sens du Mouvement*, by Alain Berthoz (1997). In his book – which refers to Poincaré's theory – Berthoz explains that the vestibular organ, found in both our inner ears and first identified in 1789, constitutes an egocentric referential, which measures the head's movements and onto which is organised our perception of movement in space.

Sense in Translation 23

Figure 2.1 Drawing of a running man by Alain Berthoz in *Le sens du mouvement* (Odile Jacob 1997) p. 111. Drawn from Muybridge phtographs with a line locating the position and angle of the vestibular organ.
Source: Alain Berthoz, *Le sens du mouvement* © Odile Jacob, 1997.

The vestibular organ is made up of three canals: the horizontal canal slightly angled at 20° above our eye line, the other two canals being at 45° to the vertical planes (one frontal cutting the body from side to side, the other sagittal, cutting the body from back to front).

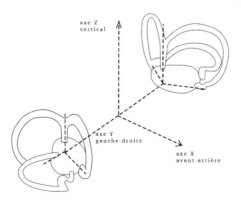

Figure 2.2 Vestibular Organ Canals, redrawn by the author from an image by ORION (Office de Recherche Interdisciplinaire sur les Organisations Neurophysiologiques).

24 *Sense in Translation*

Both these sensorial organs located on either side of the body are thus three-axis organs, measuring movement in a Euclidean referential system. Berthoz goes as far as to suggest that this particular arrangement might be at the origin of Euclidean geometry. But Poincaré doesn't equate the real world to a geometrical one, far from it, and he warns:

> [la géométrie] ne s'occupe pas en réalité des objets solides naturels, elle a pour objet certains solides idéaux, absolument invariables, qui n'en sont qu'une image simplifiée et bien lointaine.
> ([1902] 1968, 93)

> Geometry would be only the study of the movement of solid bodies; but in reality, it is not concerned with natural solids: its object is certain ideal solids, absolutely invariable, which are but a greatly simplified and very remote image of them.
> ([1905] 1952, 970)

In his chapter "L'espace et la géométrie," Poincaré compares the geometrical space to what he calls our *espace représentatif* – although the terminology can be a little misleading today, since Poincaré refers not only to visual, but also to tactile and motor perceptions as well, 'Representation' here should not to be mistaken for 'visualisation.' Representative space is totally different from geometrical space and is also a lot more complex as it involves not only our eyes but also the rest of our body and in particular he insists on our muscles which enable bodily movement. So how might geometry be of any use? Poincaré describes geometry as the study of *movements*, which is what interests us here. He makes important points about the relationship between the pure geometrical space and representative space, which is made of our sensations and perceptions in the world. According to him, we are able to locate an object in space because "we represent to ourselves the movements that must take place to reach that object" ([1905] 1952, 57); that is, we imagine the sensations of the muscular efforts we need to make in order to reach a particular object in space, at a particular distance from us. This effort will differ whether the object is located at the top of a hill or on the same horizontal plane, for instance. For Poincaré, our understanding of movement and our ability to identify movement as such is made possible because:

a. we are capable of movement ourselves and
b. we are able to observe the movement of solids.

If one of these conditions is inherent to our bodies, the other emerges out of experience. Poincaré's position, which can also be attributed to many phenomenologists, is that the notion of space cannot exist prior to our actions. Here he explains how we effectively recognise – and the word *recognise* is essential – the displacement of an object between two points:

> Suppose a solid body to occupy successively the positions α and β; in the first position it will give us an aggregate of impressions A,

Figure 2.3

> and in the second position the aggregate of impressions B.

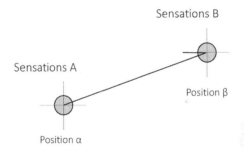

Figure 2.4

Now let there be a second solid body, of qualities entirely different from the first – of different colour, for instance.

Figure 2.5

> Assume it to pass from the position α, where it gives us the aggregate of impressions A' to the position β, where it gives us the aggregate of impressions B'.

26 *Sense in Translation*

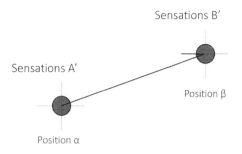

Figure 2.6

In general, the aggregate A will have nothing in common with the aggregate A', nor will the aggregate B have anything in common with the aggregate B'. The transition from the aggregate A to the aggregate B, and that of the aggregate A' to the aggregate B', are therefore two changes which 'in themselves' have in general nothing in common. Yet we consider both these changes as displacements; and, further, we consider them the 'same' displacement.

How can this be? It is simply because they may be both corrected by the 'same' *correlative movement of our body*. 'Correlative movement', therefore, constitutes the 'sole connection' between two phenomena, which otherwise we should never have dreamed of connecting.

(Poincaré [1905] 1952, 72 emphasis added)

In this long extract, translated in 1905, I would replace the word 'aggregate' (reminiscent to a concrete mix) with the word 'ensemble' or 'combination' and the word 'impression' with the word 'sensation' or 'perception.' In the 1913 translation, Halsted replaced the word 'aggregate' for 'totality,' but kept 'impression.' With this description Poincaré suggests that the process of movement is not intuitively understood as a continuum, but needs to be reasoned upon using our experience of bodily movement. This experience calls for a series of complex muscular sensations. Poincaré adds that, in themselves, those muscular sensations do not have a specific direction:

> Ce que je vois, c'est que les sensations qui correspondent à des mouvements de même direction sont liées dans mon esprit par une simple association d'idées. C'est à cette association que se ramène ce que nous appelons 'le sentiment de la direction.'
>
> (Poincaré [1902] 1968, 81)

What I do see is that the sensations which correspond to movements in the same direction are connected in my mind by a mere association of ideas. It is to this association that what we call 'the sense of direction' is reducible. This feeling therefore cannot be found in a single sensation.
(Poincaré 1913, 69)

Again here, Poincaré argues for a sense that is acquired through numerous comparative experiences, an analysis supported by the physiologist Berthoz in his book on movement. This is important in that it defines translation not simply as an arbitrary abstract construction, but also as an act which recalls our bodily experience. In other words we are able to identify the movement of external objects around us, and by extension, of people around us, only because we are able to represent the movements our own body would have to make to travel the same distance. If we see a chair being moved from one end of the room to another, we can identify this movement as translatory because we have travelled similar distances ourselves and are able to represent or recall all the muscular efforts required to travel this distance. This translatory phenomenon is a process, a construct involving various levels of representation of bodily perceptions, and absolute geometrical translation is something we are only able to understand through the correlative translatory motion of our very own body. So if linguistic translation is to carry a word from one language to another, then we might consider how linguistic translation involves a correlative translatory motion of the translator's body – between languages – that is, from one language to the other. Not only is the sense of the word altered through translation, but the act of translation itself is accompanied by a *sense* of translatory motion.

Geometry might not immediately appear to be the most appropriate route suited to investigate what I would qualify as a linguistic experience, yet the analogy is so widely accepted that one ought to investigate rather than reject. Maurice Merleau-Ponty himself – as I have also noted in Chapter 1 – insists that phenomenology's greatest achievement, in its study of the human phenomenon, is to have been able to reconcile extreme objectivism with extreme subjectivism (1945, 20), in other words, to join the sciences with the humanities. So in order to test the sense of translatory motion that accompanies linguistic translation, let us consider words as objects of scientific inquiry in the tradition of Ferdinand de Saussure's structuralist linguistic, and envisage the translation and series of associations of the word 'umbrella.' The various meanings of the word 'umbrella' were first brought to my attention by a passage in

Paul Auster's short novel *City of Glass*, part of *The New York Trilogy* (1990), where the protagonist talks about the inadequacy of language to describe the world he lives in:

> 'You see, I am in the process of inventing a new language. [...]'
> 'A new language?'
> 'Yes. A language that will at last say what we have to say. For our words no longer correspond to the world. [...]'
> 'Consider a word that refers to a thing – "umbrella", for example. When I say the word "umbrella", you see the object in your mind. You see a kind of stick, with collapsible metal spokes on top of that form an armature for a waterproof material which, when opened, will protect you from the rain.'
>
> (1990, 92–93)

When I say the word 'umbrella,' I see a small black collapsible object, smuggled in most of Londoners' bags before they go to work every morning. When I say the word *'parapluie'* however, I see the walking stick umbrella my grandfather used to prop himself with when strolling in the sun. As a bilingual speaker I also associate the word with the French word *'ombrelle,'* which protects from the sun. The shifts between one and the other languages can therefore refer to different objects and the associations are best described in the following diagrams.

When I translate the word 'umbrella' into French, I get *parapluie*; this is what Roman Jakobson ([1959] 2000) would describe as 'interlingual translation' from English to French, preserving the meaning of the word.

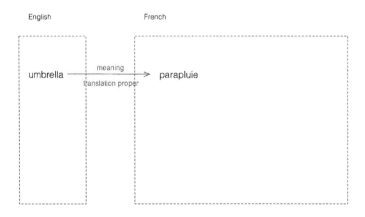

Figure 2.7

Etymologically, 'parapluie' comes from 'para,' meaning 'against,' and *pluie*, meaning 'rain.' But 'umbrella' sounds very similar to the French word *ombrelle*, and by connotation I will associate the word 'umbrella' to the word *'ombrelle.'*

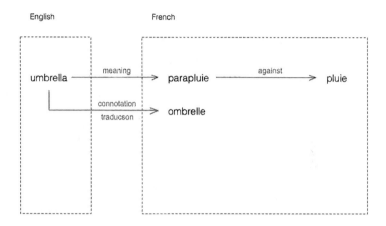

Figure 2.8

The *'ombrelle'* creates *'ombre,'* or 'shade.'

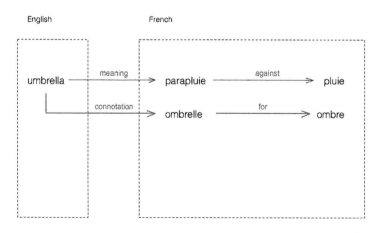

Figure 2.9

30 *Sense in Translation*

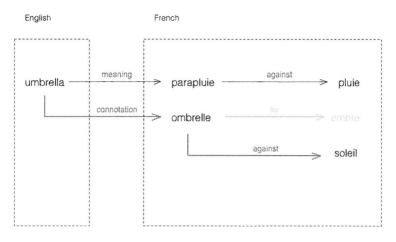

Figure 2.10

Because of the earlier transformation from '*parapluie*' to '*pluie*' using 'para' as 'against,' I will transform the word '*ombre*' and turn it into its opposite. Similarly *ombre* becomes *soleil* or 'sun.'

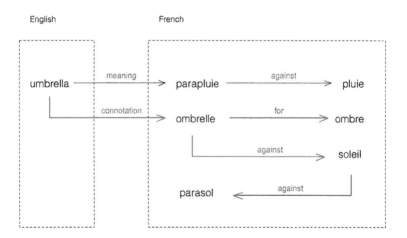

Figure 2.11

And by applying the reverse transformation once more in the opposite direction, *soleil* becomes *parasol*, against '*soleil*' or against 'sun.'

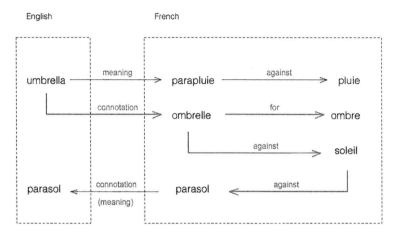

Figure 2.12

'*Parasol*' in French is a large folding device generally made of canvas you might find over garden tables to protect from the sun. The small handheld protection device against the sun is the *ombrelle*. The word '*parasol*' also belongs to the English language, so I can translate the word from French to English by homophony.

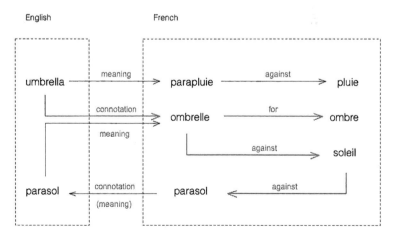

Figure 2.13

As it happens this translation by homophony is also an inter-lingual translation as 'parasol' in English is indeed a shading device that one might find over garden tables, but 'parasol' also translates, into French as *'ombrelle'* (*Larousse Grand Dictionnaire Anglais-Français / Français Anglais*, unabridged ed., s.v. "parasol").

Note that umbrella and parasol now entertain a very interesting and complex relationship. Etymologically umbrella does not come from the French though, but from the Italian *'umbrello,'* or 'sunshade.' This diagram now shows the numerous transformations words undertake, all of which I consider to be translations where the operators, or vectors may vary. This ensemble of vectors constitutes what I will call the *bilingual vector field*, or *bilingual space*. Let us now consider the appropriateness of such geometry to the bilingual experience or bilingual phenomenon, and see how the bilingual vector field is in fact a *lived* bilingual space.

In *The Origin of Geometry*, Edmund Husserl explains that geometry is commonly accepted as a tradition; he writes that in textbooks of elementary geometrical instruction we are taught to deal with *ready-made* concepts ([1939] 1989, 169). What matters to Husserl, however, is a necessary return to geometry's origin in order to give geometry its legitimacy and grant it universal and perennial status. He writes that if the original sense lies within the "subject of the inventor" and is therefore subjective, geometry exists nonetheless by way of what is "objectively there" for everyone:

> And all forms newly produced by someone on the basis of pre-given forms immediately take on the same objectivity. This is, we note, an 'ideal' objectivity. [...] In a certain way ideal objects do exist objectively in the world, but it is only by virtue of these two-levelled repetitions and ultimately in virtue of sensibly embodying repetitions.
>
> ([1939] 1989, 161)

In other words, ideal and geometrical objects owe their existence to the originary subjective sense their inventor gave to them and owe their legitimacy to the successive repetitions and reiterations by subsequent observers. However, with his return to the origin of geometry, Husserl intends neither a historical study of geometry nor an attempt to discover Thales' ancestors; he rather is searching for geometry's *fundamental* origin. In this search, Husserl explains how geometry is born out of our being in the world: surrounded by 'things,' we have established geometry from pre-existing practices of measure: surveying fields and measuring in order to build. These are active practices of the sensing body from which mathematicians or geometers eventually developed the science of geometry. For Husserl, Geometry was born out of this originary sense:

> Measuring belongs to every culture, varying only according to stages from primitive to higher perfections. We can always presuppose some measuring technique, whether of a lower or higher type, in the essential forward development of culture, [as well as] the growth of such a technique, thus also including the art of design for buildings, of surveying fields, pathways, etc., such a technique is always already there, already abundantly developed and pregiven to the philosopher who did not yet know geometry but who should be conceivable as its inventor.
> ([1939] 1989, 178)

Husserl talks about the 'sense' (German *Sinn*) of geometry. He explains that in the case of advanced geometry, this sense runs the risk of being dissociated from the practice of geometry. Where progress and logical deductions are so elaborate, the original sense, intended by its inventor, might be lost and logic and sense become dissociated. For geometry to retain its validity, its original sense needs to be reactivated at each stage of our developments in geometry. This sense, he explains is also intersubjective or universal and traverses history through what he believes to be a shared humanity.

The origin of translation however, with or without deformation, is easily reactivated. The sense of translation from A to B is elementary and, as we have seen earlier, is accompanied by the representation of correlative movement of the body. So even if the theorems of translation might have originated with an individual, its origin is still sensed and needs very little effort to be 'reactivated.' It is this original sense that I believe to be reactivated in the moving of words from one language to another: the 'sense' of geometrical translation is reactivated in the 'act' of linguistic translation.

Interestingly Husserl's entire demonstration of the origins of geometry takes its cue from language itself. He affirms that language, and in particular *langue* and its grammar, can be seen as a science of ideal objects. If they have a given common signification, the sense of these ideal objects still needs to be 'reactivated' by the individual speaking body. Husserl makes the distinction, however, between what he calls the passive awakening of the signification of a word – the most common meaning of the word – and the active awakening or 'reactivation' of meaning by the speaker as a sensing being – which calls for previous experiences the speaker associates with the word. For instance, the reactivation of the speaker's own understanding of the word umbrella, might either correspond to that of a small collapsible umbrella or that of the walking stick umbrella. Husserl describes: "There is a distinction, then, between passively understanding the expression and making it self-evident by reactivating its meaning" ([1939] 1989, 164). I would like to bring the reader's attention to the fact that the English translation *The Origin of Geometry* by John P. Leavy uses the word 'meaning' in this extract, while the French translation by Jacques Derrida uses the word '*sens*.'[3] *Sens*, here, is not simply meaning. What we reactivate is not the meaning, but sensations in tandem with meaning in order to *make sense* of the word. The reactivation of the sense of the word umbrella, for instance, will bring different results, and different sensations, for different speakers. Some will refer to the small collapsible object they regularly pack in their bag and remember how light the object felt for instance while others will refer to the walking stick umbrella, and sense its considerable weight and bulk. Both types of umbrellas will reactivate a lived sense of protection.

If one is able to reactivate the sense of a word, or an expression, what then, of the *act* of linguistic translation itself, either of inter-lingual translation, or transformation by homophony or connotation? Well, we could infer that the original sense of translation is reactivated by the speaking body during these transformations:

> In the passivity in question here, as in the case of memory, what is passively awakened can be transformed back, so to speak, into the corresponding activity: this is the capacity for reactivation that belongs originally to every human being as a speaking being.
> (Husserl [1939] 1989, 164)

Translation is not then, as Evans suggests in "Translations from Drawing to Building," simply the translatory motion of words from one language to another, but also the correlative movement of the speaking body from one word to another, from one sense to another. In the case of the bilingual speaking being, the origin of the activity of translation is always sensed and language becomes a practice where this motion is felt. If we make sense of a word by activating the sense it procures in us, it is also accompanied by the sense of translation itself. Interestingly though, the French word '*traduction*' lacks the correspondence with spatial translation, and in a way, the historical substitution of the word '*translation*' by the more recent '*traduction*' has produced a dissociation between the act of translation and its original sense of translatory motion. The original sense of *traduction* is only regained or reactivated through the process of translation of the French word '*traduction*' to the English word 'translation.'

Notes

1 Parts of this essay were initially presented at the "Language, Migration and Diaspora" International Language Symposium co-organised by Royal Irish Academy and the Dublin Institute of Technology on 2 December 2011 and at the "Translations: Exchange of Ideas" Conference organised by Cardiff University on 27 June 2013. The proceedings of the "Language, Migration and Diaspora" symposium were published online in *CALL: Irish Journal for Culture, Arts, Literature and Language*, Vol. 1 (2016) and the author wishes to thank the journal editors for the permission to reproduce in this volume extracts of the essay titled "Spatial Translations and Embodied Bilingualism."
2 Centre National de Ressources Textuelles et Lexicales. 2019. "Traduire" Accessed 17 July 2019. http://www.cnrtl.fr/etymologie/traduire
3 "La compréhension passive de l'expression se distingue donc de sa mise en évidence par réactivation du sens" (Husserl [1939] 1962, 187 translated by Jacques Derrida).

Works Cited

Auster, Paul. 1990. *The New York Trilogy*. London: Penguin books.
Berthoz, Alain. 1997. *Le sens du movement*. Paris: Odile Jacob.
Evans, Robin. 1997. *Translation from Drawing to Building and Other Essays*. London: Janet Evans and Architectural Association Publications.
Husserl, Edmund. [1939] 1962. *L'Origine de la géométrie*, translated by Jacques Derrida. Paris: Presses Universitaires de France.
———. [1939] 1989. *The Origin of Geometry*, translated by David Carr in *Edmund Husserl's 'Origin of Geometry': and Introduction/Jacques Derrida*, with a preface and afterword by John P. Leavy Jr. Lincoln: University of Nebraska Press.
Jakobson, Roman. [1959] 2000. "On Linguistic Aspects of Translation" in *The Translation Studies Reader*, edited by Lawrence Venuti. London and New York: Routledge.
Merleau-Ponty, Maurice. 1945. *Phénoménologie de la perception*. Paris: Gallimard.
Poincaré, Henri. [1902] 1968. *La Science et l'hypothèse*. Paris: Flammarion.
———. 1913. *Science and Hypothesis*, translated by George Bruce Halsted. New York: The Science Press.
———. [1905] 1952. *Science and Hypothesis*, translated by William John Greenstreet. New York: Dover Publications.

3 The Expanding Space of the Train Carriage
A Phenomenological Reading of Michel Butor's *La modification*[1]

Michel Butor, besides being one of the key early figures of the *Nouveau Roman*, is a keen traveller who enjoyed the privilege of free rail travel granted to the family members of employees of the Société Nationale des Chemins de Fer Français (SNCF). For his third novel, *La modification*, he chose a train journey to measure the distance between two cities, Paris and Rome, through the narration of the protagonist's relationship with two women: his wife in Paris and his mistress in Rome. Butor is interested not only in the *genius loci* of a place – he wrote a series of descriptions of seven cities under the title *Le génie du lieu* – but also in its relations to other places. Having lived in many different countries, he writes from experience and measures both the distances and the links between things. Visited locations are inscribed in a complex literary trajectory made of moments past, present and future. The novel is punctuated by the succession of train stations along the journey, and Butor makes interesting use of the physical or geographical distances separating them in order to test what Maurice Merleau-Ponty refers to as *lived* space.

In his essay "Le voyage et l'écriture" (1974), Butor proposes a new science to study human travel and literature which he astutely names *Itérologie*. The word itself is a sort of displacement; from the Latin *Iter* or passage, it connotes the notion of iteration or repetition of the travels through the medium of literature. If the essay touches upon something which permeates his works, it remains strangely detached from his fiction and does not attempt to analyse it explicitly. Instead, Butor sets out to list various forms of travel here and various forms of literature there, like an *inventaire à la Prévert*. But perhaps one of the prime realisations of the essay is that for him, *travelling is writing and writing is travelling*, and so by extension *reading is travelling and travelling is reading*.

Expanding Space of the Train Carriage

Gare de Lyon, Fontainebleau, Montereau, Saint-Julien-du-Sault, Joigny, Laroche-Migennes, Laumes-Alésia, Darcey, Dijon, Chevrey-Chambertin, Fontaines-Mercurey, Varennes-le-Grand, Senozan, Pont-de-Veyle, Polliat, Bourg ... the train itinerary is referred to many times throughout the novel and has subsequently been published as a timetable by Françoise Van Rossum-Guyon in *Critique du roman* (1970). There she lists more than 40 train stations and some 21 hours of travel which unfold over the 236 pages of the novel. If the itinerary covers a territory which is measurable, the narration is not limited to the visited train stations and projects us far beyond. Butor uses words – and the many surfaces of the train carriage – to *project* the reader onto other worlds and his novel performs and epitomises what Merleau-Ponty considers to be the very virtue of language, which is to *project* us to what it signifies (1969, 29). He invites the readers to take their place in the train and in the following pages we will see how the main protagonist's body – and by extension that of the reader – is put in the centre of the narrative and is a requisite to our spatial literary experience, as it is through the body that lived distances as well as our sense of movement are understood. Butor's novel starts with these words:

> Vous avez mis le pied gauche sur la rainure de cuivre, et de votre épaule droite vous essayez en vain de pousser un peu plus le panneau coulissant. Vous vous introduisez par l'étroite ouverture en vous frottant contre ses bords, puis, votre valise couverte de granuleux cuir sombre couleur d'épaisse bouteille, votre valise assez petite d'homme habitué aux longs voyages, vous l'arrachez par sa poignée collante, avec vos doigts qui se sont échauffés, si peu lourde qu'elle soit, de l'avoir portée jusqu'ici, vous la soulevez et vous sentez vos muscles et vos tendons se dessiner non seulement dans vos phalanges, dans votre paume, votre poignet et votre bras, mais dans votre épaule aussi, dans toute la moitié du dos et dans vos vertèbres depuis votre cou jusqu'aux reins.
>
> (1957, 7)

Standing with your left foot on the grooved brass sill, you try in vain with your right shoulder to push the sliding door a little wider open. You edge your way in through the narrow opening, then you lift up your suitcase of bottle-green grained leather, the smallish suitcase of a man used to making long journeys, grasping the sticky handle with fingers that are hot from having carried even so light a weight so far, and you feel the muscles and tendons tense not only in your finger-joints, the palm of your hand, your wrist and your arm, but in your shoulder too, all down one side of your back along your vertebrae from neck to loins.

(1958a, 9)

Butor's phenomenological approach to writing and reading was first brought to light by Lois Oppenheim in 1980, in her book *Intentionality and Intersubjectivity: A Phenomenological Study of Butor's La Modification*. There she reveals, having corresponded with the author about the project, that, unsurprisingly perhaps, Butor had been the pupil of both Merleau-Ponty and Gaston Bachelard and also studied Heidegger and Husserl's writings "with so much passion" (Oppenheim 1980, 8).

About the use of the second-person plural pronoun in *La modification*, Oppenheim writes that it "assumes the presence of the reader," who becomes not only "the accomplice in the action of the novel, but in a sense, is named as the protagonist as well" (1980, 31). But this *vous*, entering the train, is not just the main protagonist; he is an *embodied* protagonist. In these first few lines, Butor refers to your left foot, your right shoulder, your fingers, muscles, tendons, phalanxes, your palm, wrist and arm, shoulder again, half your back, vertebrae, neck and kidneys, bringing awareness to the reader's entire body by enumerating every part of it from foot to neck. This body, our body, is essential to the understanding of space, and, as Merleau-Ponty puts it, "there would be no space at all for me if I had no body" (1962, 102), and despite evincing a lifelong fascination for Descartes' work on optics and geometry, he writes:

L'espace n'est plus celui dont parle la Dioptrique, réseau de relations entre objets, tel que le verrait un tiers témoin de ma vision, ou un géomètre qui la reconstruit et la survole, c'est un espace compté à partir de moi comme point zéro de la spatialité. Je ne le vois pas selon son enveloppe extérieure, je le vis du dedans, j'y suis englobé. Après tout, le monde est autour de moi, non devant moi.

(1964a, 59)

Space is no longer what it was in the Dioptric, a network of relations between objects such as would be seen by a witness to my vision or by a geometer looking over it and reconstructing it from outside. It is, rather, a space reckoned starting from me as the zero point or degree zero of spatiality. I do not see it according to its exterior envelope; I live in it from the inside; I am immersed in it. After all, the world is all around me, not in front of me.

(1964b, 178)

So if space is assessed from the body as point zero, in the opening sentence of *La modification*, Butor puts the reader of the novel himself in the zero position by dint of the first word "vous," and its recurrence "vous vous" at the start of the second sentence. Thus the reader's body becomes the point zero of reference for the ensuing spatial experience which the novel unfolds.

"L'espace du roman," an essay published seven years after *La modification*, in 1964, is instrumental in articulating Butor's conception of space. For him, the space of the novel is also a lived space which starts from, and extends to, the space of reading. Thus the sofa in your living room, the chair in the library or the seat in the train where you might be reading the novel becomes points of departure for the space of the novel. In Butor's work, the reader's body is this point of departure. It is the point from which all distances are measured, as I will show in the first part of this chapter, as well as the place where movement is felt, or 'lived.'

Additionally it is worth noting a number of significant geographical specificities: first, the French rail network spreads over the country radially from Paris, with all trains departing from the capital city and, second, all distances to and from Paris on road signs and maps are measured from a specific point on the Parvis de Notre Dame on the Ile de la Cité, called the *point zéro des routes de France*, or *point kilomètrique zéro* (point zero of the road system in France or the kilometric point zero). Butor's novel starts with the body as point zero of the spatial experience, departing from the geographical point zero in France.

The first few pages of *La modification* are about settling into the train compartment at the Gare de Lyon, then checking the time on the platform clock and correcting it on your watch, then seeing the neighbouring train set off, and finally feeling the departure of your own train through a jolt of your own rather strained back (Butor 1957, 12). The movement of the train is not viewed from the outside, it is not simply observed like that of the neighbouring train, but the stress is, once more, put onto the protagonist and the reader's own body. The jolt that we feel tells us that we are moving; we are not calling on any muscular effort to set our body in motion like we would for walking, yet we are *in motion* on the train. The movement is a relative movement of displacement, which, although it does not call for any particular muscular effort, the author insists is felt through our body. This distinction is important and we will see later how being *in movement* and actually *moving* relate to a form of *literary* movement.

Butor wrote *La modification* in Switzerland, where he was teaching French Literature, as well as History and Geography, subjects he was not familiar with at the time, to secondary school students in Geneva. He spent some time preparing for this new assignment, which might explain why the novel is imbued with numerous descriptions of key buildings and monuments, complete with precise historical and geographical details. Butor's interest in and fascination for cities is obvious but he could only write about one city when he had distanced himself from it: he would write about a city from another one.

> J'étais fasciné par les villes, je le suis toujours, mais j'ai pris un recul différent. Pour mieux voir et réfléchir, j'avais besoin de parler d'une ville depuis une autre. Ainsi j'ai écrit *Passage de Milan*, étude sur Paris, quand j'étais en Angleterre. *L'Emploi du temps*, qui se déroule en Angleterre, a été écrit à Paris et en Grèce.
>
> (Butor 2006, 58)

> I was fascinated by cities, and still am, but have a different outlook now. In order to see better and understand, I needed to talk about a city from another one. Thus, I wrote *Passage de Milan*, study on Paris, when I was in England. *L'emploi du temps*, which is set in England, was written in Paris and in Greece.
>
> (trans. my own)

Butor travelled and lived in many different countries and eventually settled in Lucinges, Haute Savoie, not very far from Geneva, in a house he named *A l'écart*, meaning 'away from,' as if to put some distance between himself and the rest of the world.

We have seen that Butor in *La modification* makes use of explicit physical distances throughout the train journey as listed by Françoise Van Rossum-Guyon – although here the emphasis is on time when the distance between cities could also be expressed in kilometres. However, Butor, if he mentions the various train stations in the course of the narration, really uses those geographical distances in order to test the *lived* distances described by Merleau-Ponty:

> Outre la distance physique ou géométrique qui existe entre moi et toutes choses, une distance vécue me relie aux choses qui comptent et existent pour moi et les relie entre elles.
>
> (1945, 338)

> Besides the physical and geometrical distance which stands between myself and all things, a 'lived' distance binds me to things which count and exist for me, and links them to each other.
>
> (1962, 333)

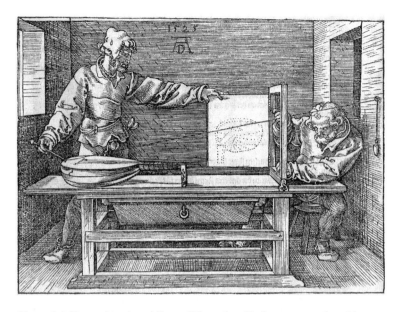

Figure 3.1 Engraving by Albert Dürer in *Underweysung der Messung* (Nuremberg 1525).

If we see a village in the distance, consisting of a church spire and a few houses, we can approximately tell the distance which separates us from the village, as well as the distance between the church and the other houses, yet we cannot deduce this distance from what we see alone. The image captured by our eyes is very much like that of a screen, and the distances can only be assessed because of our previous experience of movement. Because we are able to experience distances, that is, move from one side of the room to the other, we are able to appreciate distances between ourselves and things as well as between things. We know the distance which separates us from the village because we have travelled similar distances before.

Butor's lived distances are expressed by the manipulation of those physical distances through various techniques borrowed from painting, photography and filmmaking. It should on this occasion be noted that Butor has worked with an impressive number of artists throughout his writing carrier, mostly photographers and painters – curiously, it seems, no filmmakers – and has produced over a thousand artists' books. He is therefore no stranger to these artistic practices and embraces them wholeheartedly. In "L'espace du roman," he compares the novelist to a painter and writes:

> Plantant son chevalet ou sa caméra dans un des points de l'espace évoqué, le romancier retrouvera tous les problèmes de cadrage, de composition et de perspective que rencontre le peintre. Comme lui, il pourra choisir entre un certain nombre de procédés pour exprimer la profondeur, l'un des plus simples étant la superposition claire de plusieurs de ces vues immobiles.
>
> (1964, 53)

> Planting his easel or his camera in one of the parts of the space evoked, the novelist will rediscover all the problems of framing, of composition, and of perspective encountered by the painter. Like him, he may choose among a certain number of methods in order to express depth, one of the simplest being the obvious superimposition of several of these motionless views.
>
> (1970, 34)

In an interview, Butor (2008) notes that the writers associated with the movement of the Nouveau Roman were greatly aware that cinema had changed the way we see and perceive the world. He makes no secret of the use of cinematographic techniques in his work. I would, in this instance, question the translation of the French *caméra* into the English 'camera' as he is probably referring to the moving image and the film camera – and not the *appareil photo*. We will see in the second part of this chapter how Butor depicts movement in the novel, but let us first bring our attention to the way in which he projects objects and people alike, located at various distances or depths, onto a single plane in the following extract:

> De retour à votre compartiment de première classe où vous étiez seul, apercevant la mer de temps en temps, vous avez repris les lettres de Julien l'Apostat que vous aviez laissées sur l'étagère, mais vous avez gardé le livre entre vos mains sans l'ouvrir, regardant passer la gare de Tarquinia et la ville au loin avec ses tours grises devant les montagnes arides, par la fenêtre ouverte qui laissait entrer quelquefois une bouffée de sable avec l'air frais, puis fixant cette tache de soleil en forme de couperet qui s'étalait de plus en plus grande sur l'un des coussins.
>
> (1957, 205)

Back in your first class compartment where you were alone, with an occasional glimpse of the sea, you took up once more the Letters of Julian the Apostate, which you had left on the shelf, but you held the book in your hands without opening it, looking out through the open window which sometimes let in a whiff of sand or the cool breeze, and watching the station of Tarquinia go by and the town in the distance with its grey towers outlined against the arid mountains, then staring at the wedge-shaped patch of sunlight that was gradually spreading over one of the cushions.
(1958a, 190)

Here, Butor gives us the immensity of the sea, the empire of Julian the Apostate, Tarquinia's train station, the grey town in the distance and the cushion of the seat in front of us, all in the space of a single sentence, as if to eventually flatten all distances into a single picture, a single plane. He uses the train window like the painter might use the surface of the canvas or the photographer his photosensitive film, but he also makes use of the architecture of the train carriage *à compartiments* and its many surfaces. The train carriage is divided up into smaller compartments of six passengers distributed along a side corridor, and all the division panels would have windows through which you can see the adjacent space.

En face de vous, entre l'ecclésiastique et la jeune femme gracieuse et tendre, à travers la vitre, à travers une autre vitre, vous apercevez assez distinctement l'intérieur d'un autre wagon de modèle plus ancien aux bancs de bois jaune, aux filets de ficelle, dans la pénombre au-delà des reflets composés, un homme de la même taille que vous, dont vous ne sauriez ni préciser l'âge, ni décrire avec exactitude les vêtements, qui reproduit avec plus de lenteur encore les gestes fatigués que vous venez d'accomplir.
(1957, 10)

Opposite you, between the cleric and the graceful, gentle young woman, through one window and another window beyond it, you can dimly make out, in another less up-to-date coach with yellow wooden seats and string racks, in the half darkness beyond the composite reflections, a man of your height, whose exact age you could not guess and whose clothes you could not describe with any precision, reproducing even more slowly than yourself the weary movements you have just made.
(1958a, 12)

Furthermore, some of those surfaces also have mirrors and indeed the previous extract in which the man in front repeats "your own" movements may be seen as a *delayed* mirror. Lucien Dallenbach writes extensively about Butor's use of mirrors in *Le récit spéculaire* (Dallenbach 1977, 16). He describes the use of mirrors as a process of mise en abyme and interprets them as signs and symbols, which were often associated with the Nouveau Roman at the time. But he also explicitly rejects upfront any reference to the idea of depth, infinity or vertigo in his analysis, which I think are quintessential to Butor's work. Butor is very precise in his descriptions; in the above extract, for instance, the man seen through layers of glass in the compartment ahead is of the exact same height as the main protagonist, and repeats the exact same movements in the distance.

For Merleau-Ponty, depth is the most "existential" dimension as, contrary to height and width, it is not registered on the eye's retina, and is the result of our experience of space.

> [La profondeur] est, pour ainsi dire, de toutes les dimensions, la plus "existentielle", parce que – c'est ce qu'il y a de vrai dans l'argument de Berkeley – elle ne se marque pas sur l'objet lui-même, elle appartient de toute évidence à la perspective et non aux choses [...] elle annonce un certain lien indissoluble entre les choses et moi par lequel je suis situé devant elles, tandis que la largeur peut, à première vue, passer pour une relation entre les choses elles-mêmes où le sujet percevant n'est pas impliqué.
> (1945, 305)

> [Depth] is, so to speak, the most 'existential' of all dimensions, because (and here Berkeley's argument is right) it is not impressed upon the object itself, it quite clearly belongs to the perspective and not to things. [...] It announces a certain indissoluble link between things and myself by which I am placed in front of them, whereas breadth can, at first sight, pass for a relationship between things themselves, in which the perceiving subject is not implied.
> (1962, 298)

As noted earlier, the image captured by our eyes is a single image, very much like that of a screen, without any indication of depth. An object in the distance will appear to our eye smaller than it really is and we can only infer its true dimensions by assessing its distance from us. Merleau-Ponty shows a certain admiration for the work of

Expanding Space of the Train Carriage 45

Descartes on optics, which he often returns to. For Merleau-Ponty, it is the effort of convergence our eyes need to make in order to see the object in focus which enables us to assess this distance. From the rotation angle of our eyes reaching the object, we conclude its distance from us and effectively take note of our relationship and motivation to the object.

However, limiting our understanding of depth and distances to our eyes alone seems rather reductive and neglects the complexity of our bodily and spatial experience. In *Phénoménologie de la perception*, Merleau-Ponty dedicates a whole chapter to what he calls "La spatialité du corps propre et la motricité," translated as "The Spatiality of One's own Body and Motricity," where he shows that our understanding of space is the result of our experience of movement. For him, "it is clearly in action that the spatiality of the body is brought about, and the analysis of movement itself should allow us to understand spatiality better" (2012, 105).

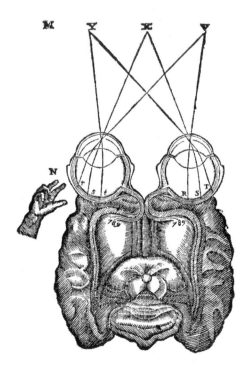

Figure 3.2 Engraving in René Descartes's *Discours de la méthode* (Paris: Théodore Girard, 1667).

Recent neurological studies confirm this idea and, in his book *Le sens du mouvement*, physiologist Alain Berthoz (1997) explains how various parts of the body are involved in spatial cognition and also, of course, our sense of movement. He repeatedly acknowledges the relevance of Merleau-Ponty's theories and also refers to Henri Poincaré, whose essays on the philosophy of science are particularly enlightening as we have seen in Chapter 2. Poincaré clearly demonstrates the idea, which Berthoz later validates, that to localise an object in space *"we represent to ourselves the movements that must take place to reach that object"* (1905, 67; italics original), that is, we imagine the sensations of the muscular efforts we would have to make to get to the object. Our understanding of space is not purely regulated by optical laws, it is also produced by motor activity and we take measure of our relation to things through bodily sensations.

In parenthesis I would like to note the relevance of the imperial measuring system. It uses feet and inches, that is, bodily units, rather than the somehow remote ten-millionth part of one-quarter of the meridian as a unit of measure, which is the basis of the metric system. The metre, which no longer takes the body as a frame of reference but the earth on which we live, is the result of an empirical strategy in which the earth becomes the object of study and the focus of investigations, but where we ultimately forget our relationship to it. The foot, in comparison, constitutes not only a bodily unit of reference, but it is also in direct contact with the earth it measures. The foot, as well as being a measuring unit, is also mobile and related to motor activity.

So we have seen that taking measure of distances calls for an active participation of the reader to reach that which is described and involves more than vision alone; it calls for an active *effort* on the part of the reader. When we see the grey town in the distance, beyond the station of Tarquinia, not only do our eyes converge, but we also *represent* the *muscular efforts* necessary to reach [rejoindre] the town, we make what I will call, for the time being, an *effort of projection*.

After having published *La modification*, Butor decided to abandon the novel to the dismay of his publishers, and also distanced himself from the literary movement of the *Nouveau Roman*, preferring instead to embrace other forms of writing. But in the essay "L'espace du roman", published a few years later in 1964, he writes that every novel is in fact a form of travel:

> Toute fiction s'inscrit donc en notre espace comme voyage, et l'on peut dire à cet égard que c'est là le thème fondamental de toute littérature romanesque; tout roman qui nous raconte un

voyage est donc plus clair, plus explicite que celui qui n'est pas capable d'exprimer métaphoriquement cette distance entre le lieu de la lecture et celui où nous emmène le récit.

(1964, 50)

All fiction, then, is inscribed in our space as a voyage, and we may say in this regard that this is the fundamental theme of all novels; every novel which describes a journey is thus clearer, more explicit, than one which is not capable of expressing metaphorically that distance.

(1970, 32)

Butor's choice of the train journey for *La modification* can be seen as a direct application of the novel as travel, yet his essay introduces another travelling dimension: it establishes a link between the place of reading and the place where the story takes us. Butor explains how at the time of reading a spatial translation or displacement of the reader occurs. But what follows is more intriguing, if not slightly puzzling. In the next paragraph he writes:

A partir du moment où le lointain me devient proche, c'est ce qui était proche qui prend le pouvoir du lointain, qui m'apparaît comme encore plus lointain.

(1964, 50)

The moment what is distant becomes near to me, it is what was near that assumes the power of what was distant, that seems even more distant to me.

(1970, 33)

The analogy with the *mise au point* or focal adjustment of a camera springs to mind, with its ability to focus on what is far whilst rendering what is near blurry and vice versa. But as we have seen earlier in this chapter, the shift between what is near and what is far is not purely visual but also involves an effort of projection on the part of the reader, who will represent to himself the muscular efforts required to reach a certain point. If we project ourselves to the village in the distance, we 'forget' about our immediate surroundings; we effectively shift our frame of reference from the chair we sit on to that new point in the distance, which, in turn, becomes the new point zero of reference. Once we locate our own body in the village, all new measures are taken from that new point of departure.

In *Intentionality and Intersubjectivity*, Oppenheim suggests that the reader experiences two types of spatial displacements: one which she claims is *outside* the text, whilst the other is *inside* the text (1980, 87). I would argue that there is no such clear distinction between displacement outside and inside the text and instead would suggest considering the successive shifts of frame of reference in the act of reading as a continuous series of *repositionings*, much like the various stops of an itinerary.

Eventually the distance, as Butor explains, is measured between the reader and the text and we have seen that a displacement within the text involves a repositioning of the reader, which is felt through his body if he is to be spatially aware. So the reader or, in the case of *La modification, you* travel and project yourself from your chair to the city of Rome and, throughout the story, a succession of shifts and repositionings occur from your place of reading and back again. You follow an itinerary, a certain trajectory.

A distinction between various types of displacements, however, may be seen in the *effectuation* of movement and muscular effort as opposed to their *representation*. The reader keeps moving whether inside or outside the text, and whether he be physically moving or not. Some movements require muscular effort, others the *representation* of muscular effort, whilst others still require no effort at all. Instead of the categorisation proposed by Butor for his *Itérologie* – where he writes about nomadism, exodus, emigration, the return trip, the leisure trip, the business trip, the foreign country, the return to the home country or pilgrimages – I therefore suggest studying movements according to their degree of *effort*.

Merleau-Ponty in *Phénoménologie de la perception* marks a distinction between relative movement and absolute movement, and concludes that it is our ability to shift between frames of reference which enables us to experience relative movement: "The relativity of movement is reduced to the power we have of changing domains within the large world" (2012, 293). Merleau-Ponty uses the words 'domain' and, in the following sentence, 'milieu,' which are indeterminate and do not necessarily reflect the egocentric nature of the phenomenon. When we change position, we do not simply enter a pre-existing milieu but create a new environment, with new relationships with the surrounding elements, which is unique and particular to us. For this reason I would rather use the term 'frame of reference,' and centre that frame – here not intended as two-dimensional but multi-dimensional – on the body. Merleau-Ponty further uses the word 'power,' which seems stronger than 'ability' and also suggests a degree of intentionality. To explain this notion, he writes about the movement of the train:

> Je peux voir à volonté mon train ou le train voisin en mouvement si je ne fais rien ou si je m'interroge sur les illusions du mouvement. Mais "quand je joue aux cartes dans mon compartiment, je vois bouger le train voisin, même si c'est en réalité le mien qui part; quand je regarde l'autre train et que j'y cherche quelqu'un, c'est alors mon propre train qui démarre". Le compartiment où nous avons élu domicile est "en repos", ses parois sont "verticales" et le paysage défile devant nous, dans une côte les sapins vus à travers la fenêtre nous apparaissent obliques.
>
> (1945, 331)

> I am free to see my train or the neighboring train moving, whether I do nothing or whether I examine myself on the illusions of movement. But: "When I am playing cards in my compartment, I see the train move on the next track even if it is in reality my own train which is moving, but when I am looking at the other train, searching perhaps for an acquaintance in the coach, then it is my own train that seems to be moving." The compartment where we take up residence is "at rest", its walls are "vertical", and the landscape passes by in front of us; on one side the fir trees seen through the window appear to us as diagonal.
>
> (2012, 292)

Merleau-Ponty's description of the train in movement, in which he quotes psychologist Kurt Koffka, is one many readers will have experienced. Here he proposes an explanation of the phenomenon, which I would like to expand upon and relate to our reading of *La modification*. We have already seen how Butor deals with the departure of the train at the Gare de Lyon in Paris; how the protagonist first settles in the train carriage; how the departure is felt through the protagonist's body instead of being described purely visually. We see now why 'settling in' is such an essential phase to the spatial experience and appreciation of movement. By settling into the carriage, Butor invites the reader to move away from his place of reading and take his place in the carriage, which itself is about to move. He has invited you to shift your frame of reference onto the train. But in the end, we can equally see the train of Leon Delmont, the main character, moving, or the landscape in the window moving, depending on whether we choose to return to the chair we are reading in or remain in Leon's seat in the carriage, whether we *feel* our body on the chair in the library or whether we *feel* that it is in the carriage. This shift is exemplified in the following extract:

> De l'autre côté du corridor, une onze chevaux noire démarre devant une église, suit une route qui longe la voie, rivalise avec vous de vitesse, se rapproche, s'éloigne, disparaît derrière un bois, reparaît, traverse un petit fleuve avec ses saules et une barque abandonnée, se laisse distancer, rattrape le chemin perdu, puis s'arrête à un carrefour, tourne et s'enfuit vers un village dont le clocher bientôt s'efface derrière un repli de terrain. Passe la gare de Montereau.
>
> (1957, 20)

> Beyond the corridor, a small black car starts off in front of a church, follows a road alongside the railway, races the train, draws near, moves away, disappears behind a wood, reappears, crosses a little river with willow trees and a deserted boat, drops behind, catches up, then halts at a cross-road, turns off and escapes towards a village the steeple of which soon vanishes behind a fold of land. Montereau station has gone by.
>
> (1958a, 20)

Here, Butor uses the cinematic technique of the 'cut' to splice two 'shots' together when the dynamic landscape suddenly gives way to Montereau station. The *onze chevaux* is the subject of the first sentence, and to understand its movement, we need to make an effort of projection, take a seat in the car and drive alongside the tracks, but in the same breath, we are briefly reminded ("rivalise avec vous de vitesse") that we are in fact in the train and that the train is moving; the reminder is short-lived, though, and we find ourselves back on the road.

Passe la gare de Montereau. This sentence is the last of the paragraph and produces a strange feeling. In itself the statement is not unusual and could easily be read and understood, although, of course, we know that the train station itself does not move. The uncanny feeling comes from the fact that one's position has abruptly and surreptitiously shifted. Consecutive shifts of the point of reference have taken place in this paragraph. The train station, which we know to be static, is presented as moving; this can only mean that we have moved back into the carriage, which is rendered as static, immobile,

Expanding Space of the Train Carriage 51

for this is where the author wants us to take residence again. The shift is abrupt, brutal, and requires an active participation from the reader. What appears like a simple juxtaposition of times and places actually demands of the reader an effort of translation, of readjustment, of repositioning. The effort we make to move between the outside of the train and back into the carriage is contained in the effort we make to move between (and even within) paragraphs. The novel is awash with these juxtapositions, carefully crafted along specific patterns, and with each and every new paragraph the reader undergoes yet a further spatial displacement.

Finally, the distinction between relative and absolute movement referred to by Merleau-Ponty has become hazy, for every movement, relative or absolute, is lived and felt through our own body, whether it be through direct effective effort or through an effort of projection. Movement, as Merleau-Ponty has shown, is never inherent to an object and is understood, as Poincaré notes, through 'correlative' movement of the viewer, so one might argue that there is no absolute movement and only a plethora of relative movements.

In *Phénoménologie de la perception*, Merleau-Ponty notes that some subjects suffering from cerebral pathologies lack the essential ability to imagine themselves elsewhere or are unable to 'mime' a simple action – of cutting a piece of paper with scissors, for instance, when they are perfectly able to cut it if they hold the scissors in their hand. Merleau-Ponty infers that the normal subject has the ability to 'project' himself into a situation, whether it be in time or space:

> La fonction normale qui rend possible le mouvement abstrait est une fonction de "projection" par laquelle le sujet du mouvement ménage devant lui un espace libre où ce qui n'existe pas naturellement puisse prendre un semblant d'existence.
> (1945, 142)

> The normal function that makes abstract movement possible is a function of "projection" by which the subject of movement organizes before himself a free space in which things that do not exist naturally can take on a semblance of existence.
> (2012, 114)

Beyond the window, Butor develops [*ménage*] a space where the reader is able to project himself. So by measuring the distance which separates him from the town of Tarquinia, the reader is also able to reach it [*la rejoindre*], to *join it in the distance*, and the gust of sand which enters the compartment no doubt adds to the sensory experience. The juxtapositions and manipulations of distances that were referred to in the earlier parts of this chapter are pushed to their paroxysm when, towards the end of the novel, Butor proposes to *actually* superimpose the cities of Rome and Paris, one under the ground of the other, linked to one another by a series of hatches (1957, 280).

This new geographic paradigm in which the two cities are directly connected is the result of the realisation by the author that the world has lost its centre, that the Roman Empire is no more and that Paris has lost its lustre. The psychological shift described in the book as the main protagonist decides against his initial plan to abandon his wife live and with his mistress is in fact accompanied by an important geographical shift. *La modification* is above all a spatial – and temporal – modification in which distances are problematised. When Butor finally decides against his radical scheme to superimpose the two cities, he argues that the distance between them is essential and should be kept. The distance travelled is not only part of the experience, but it has also made the experience of travelling possible. Without the distance, there would be no train journey, without the distance there would be no book: the novel would not exist, nor would the idea of it. The distance has made the book happen. *La modification* ends with these words:

> Le mieux, sans doute, serait de conserver à ces deux villes leur relations géographiques réelles et de tenter de faire revivre sur le mode de la lecture cet épisode crucial de votre aventure, le mouvement qui s'est produit dans votre esprit accompagnant le déplacement de votre corps d'une gare à l'autre à travers tous les paysages intermédiaires, vers ce livre futur et nécessaire dont vous tenez la forme dans votre main.
>
> Le couloir est vide. Vous regardez la foule sur le quai. Vous quittez le compartiment.
>
> (1957, 285–286)

The best thing, surely, would be to preserve the actual geographical relationship between these two cities, and to try and bring to life in the form of literature this crucial episode in your experience, the movement that went on in your mind while your body was being transferred from one station to another through all the intermediate landscapes, towards this book, this future necessary book of which you're holding in your hand the outward form.

The corridor is empty. You look at the crowd of people on the platform. You go out of the compartment.

(1958a, 264)

So the journey will take the form of the book, the form of the novel, the novel as travel. And again, in the last sentence of the novel, the spatial paradigm is brought back to the reader, point zero of the spatial paradigm. We leave the compartment to return to the space of reading, and Butor leaves the novel to explore other forms of writing.

Note

1 An earlier version of this essay was delivered on 1 December 2013 at the "Travelling Narratives: Modernity and the Spatial Imaginary" Symposium, organised by the English Department of the University of Zurich. The extended version presented here was then published by Routledge in 2018 in *Spatial Modernities: Geography, Narrative, Imaginaries* edited by Johannes Riquet and Elizabeth Kollmann. The author would like to thank the publishers for the permission to reprint the essay in this volume as it constitutes a pivotal point of the research.

Works Cited

Berthoz, Alain. 1997. *Le sens du mouvement*. Paris: Odile Jacob.
Butor, Michel. 1957. *La modification*. Paris: Editions de Minuit.
———. 1958a. *Second Thoughts*, translated by Jean Stewart. London: Faber & Faber.
———. 1958b. *Le génie du lieu*. Paris: Grasset.
———. 1964. *L'espace du roman*. Paris: Les Editions de Minuit.
———. 1970. *The Space of the Novel*, translated by G. Fabian. London: Jonathan Cape.
———. 1974. "Le voyage et l'écriture" in *Répertoire IV*. Paris: Les Editions de Minuit.
———. 2006. *Michel Butor: L'écriture nomade*, edited by Marie Odile Germain and Marie Minssieux-Chamonard. Paris: Bibliothèque Nationale de France.
———. 2008. TV interview with Sumana Sinha. Auteurs TV.
Dallenbach, Lucien. 1977. *Le récit spéculaire*. Paris: Editions du Seuil.
Merleau-Ponty, Maurice. 1945. *Phénoménologie de la perception*. Paris: Gallimard.
———. 1962. *Phenomenology of Perception*, translated by Colin Smith. London: Routledge.
———. 1964a. *L'œil et l'esprit*. Paris: Gallimard.

———. 1964b. 'Eye and Mind' in *The Primacy of Perception and other Essays on Phenomenological Psychology*, edited by James M. Edie and translated by Carleton Dallery. Evanston: Northwestern University Press.
———. 1969. *La prose du monde*. Paris: Gallimard.
———. 2012. *Phenomenology of Perceptio*, translated by Donald A. Landes. London: Routledge.
Oppenheim, Lois. 1980. *Intentionality and Intersubjectivity: A Phenomenological Study of Butor's La modification*. Lexington: French Forum Publishers.
Poincaré, Henri. 1905. *Science and Hypothesis*. London and Newcastle on Tyne: The Walter Scott Publishing Co. Ltd.
Van Rossum-Guyon, Françoise. 1970. *Critique du roman: essai sur La Modification de Michel Butor*. Paris: Gallimard.

4 Making Sense of Caroline Bergvall's Poetry

The Space between *les langues* and Lecercle's *Philosophy of Nonsense*[1]

I would like to start with the following words:

> Let us go to the school of writing, where we'll spend three school days initiating ourselves in the strange science of writing, which is a science of farewells. Of reunitings.
> I will begin with: **H**
> This is what writing is.
> I speak to you today (today April 24, 1990, today June 24, 1990) through two languages. From one day to another, from one page to the other, writing changes languages. I have thought certain mysteries in the French language that I cannot think in English. This loss and this gain are in writing too. I have drawn the **H**. You will have recognized it depending on which language you are immersed in. This is what writing is: **I**
> One language, **I** another language, and between the two, the line that makes them vibrate; writing forms a passageway between two shores.
>
> (Cixous 1993, 3)

It gives me great pleasure to read those lines today (19 September 2014). Their relevance to what I am about to say, I am sure, will soon become apparent. But it leaves me a little guilt as well, guilty of theft of lines that are not mine; they are Hélène Cixous' lines. They were the opening lines of Cixous' lecture at the Wellek Library, University of California, delivered in May 1990, later to be published under the title *Three Steps on the Ladder of Writing*. The lecture, the first of a series of three, was presented under the framework of Critical Theory, and yet it is so much more than theory, it is poetry, as Jacques Derrida notes on the back cover of the publication:

> Hélène Cixous is today, in my view, the greatest writer in what I will call my language, the French language if you like. And

I am weighing my words as I say that. For a great writer must be a poet-thinker, very much a poet and a very thinking poet.

If the book *Three Steps on the Ladder of Writing* is assigned to the field of critical theory, it can also be described as a piece of creative critical theory or critical poetry. From the outset however, Cixous refers to a single word: 'Writing.' Through the format of the lectures, the performative dimension of language is brought to the fore, reminiscent of Derrida's *'différance,'* (Derrida 1972) where the emphasis is put on the disjunction between written and spoken language. The lectures were first written in French by Cixous, then translated into English by Sarah Cornell and Susan Sellers, before being delivered by Cixous in English at the University of California, and finally published in English by Columbia University Press. In this short opening extract, Cixous gives us the temporal and spatial shifts that occur not only between the spoken and written word, but also the shifts that occur between one and another language. She writes and talks about the loss and gain that are made possible by the use of the written and spoken word as well as the use of two languages. Incidentally, although she does not refer to it in her lecture, the writing has also most certainly lost and gained through the translation process between the author and her translators.

Cixous' writing highlights the performative dimension of language, what French linguist Jean-Jacques Lecercle refers to as 'language that speaks us.' Throughout his work and in particular in his book *The Violence of Language* (1990), Lecercle calls for the study of 'language that speaks us' as well as 'language that we speak.' For him the speaker finds itself in the inevitable predicament of being torn between those two positions, one in which we use language, or a specific *langue*, to express something using the common meaning of the words, and the other in which language is in excess of what we intend to say. The distinction between *language that speaks us* and *language that we speak* can also be found in the work of Maurice Merleau-Ponty who distinguishes *langage parlé* et *langage parlant*. For Merleau-Ponty the distinction resides in the relationship between language and *sens* (meaning); on the one hand, the meaning of words is presupposed, whereas on the other, it takes shape at the moment it is uttered and perceived; meaning emerges, is perceived and *incorporated* at the moment of expression:

> Disons qu'il y a deux langages: le langage après coup, celui qui est acquis, et qui disparaît devant le sens dont il est devenu

porteur, – et celui qui se fait dans le moment de l'expression, qui va justement me faire glisser des signes au sens, – le langage parlé et le langage parlant.

(1969, 17)

We may say that there are two languages. First there is language after the fact, or language as an institution, which effaces itself in order to yield the meaning which it conveys. Second, there is the language which creates itself in its expressive acts, which sweeps me on from the signs toward meaning – sedimented language and speech.

(1973, 10)

It is this very *glissement* or drift into meaning that I feel applies to the reading of multilingual poetry. Caroline Bergvall is a French-Norwegian poet, based in the cities of London and Geneva. She works across artforms and media, writing in English, French, Norwegian, or across languages, for at times these are mixed, truncated and collaged. At times almost nonsensical, yet nearly always political, her writing is one I would call guttural. Her language comes from the body, it resonates. In her short text "Cat in the Throat," Bergvall writes about the friction inside the speaker's mouth:

> A lingual event is taking place, not in the voice but in the clearing of the throat.
> Spitting out the most intimate and the most naturalized source language, so-called mother tongue, is a dare, it is dangerous. It starts a whole process of re-embodying one's language spaces.
> The spittle can be resistant, unpleasant, potentially as well-aimed as a thrown shoe. Beckett's traffic from English to French is an expectoration of the English language's occupation of the colonized Irish body. His leitmotivs of speech loss, language stutter, assisted memory, gestural language all point to his fighting off one language with another language, transforming in the process both the spat-out source language and the adoptive language.
> In French, to clear one's throat is to have a cat in the throat, avoir un chat dans la gorge. One needs to spit out a cat to clear one's throat. Literally, 'un crachat' is a spittle.

(2011, 156)

The violence in this text is obvious, and shows the struggle of the bilingual speaking subject. I have noted in Chapter 1 that Saussure's term *'langue'* – or system of signs used by a group of individuals to communicate amongst themselves – the word *'langue'* also means 'tongue' – in French as well as in English, where we speak of 'mother tongue.' Bergvall's text is a reminder that the *langue*, which Saussure tried to assign to the dictionary and to institutions, belongs in fact to the speaker's body, but that *langue* can also be spat out.

Parole, which loosely translates as *speech*, draws us closer to the corporeity of language that Merleau-Ponty insists on. Both Bergvall and Lecercle consider language as a physical and bodily experience, something that comes from the body as *parole*, spreads and scatters, but which also can be violent and uncontrollable. The act of speaking, as we can see in Bergvall's poetry, can be violent. Lecercle studies a particular kind of *parole*, one that is considered odd and sits outside of the traditional literary canons. He calls it 'the remainder.' The remainder does not exist in the Saussurean tradition but takes its cues from Jacques Lacan's 'Lalangue' and Deleuze's philosophy of language. Lecercle explains:

> There is another side to language, one that escapes the linguist's attention […]. This dark side emerges in nonsensical and poetic texts, in the illuminations of mystics and the delirium of logophiliacs or mental patients.
>
> (1990, 6)

In fact, these texts of poetical euphoria, in their excesses, articulate better than anything else the workings of language. Lecercle studies the work of writers such as Louis Wolfson, Jean-Pierre Brisset and Lewis Carroll and shows that what seems eccentric potentially lies at the heart of human language. The study of these texts acts like a magnifying glass in revealing the workings of language in general. It is language pushed to its limits. It is interesting to note the similarity of approach in Merleau-Ponty's work in *Phénoménologie de la perception*, where he observes the behaviour of patients with pathological disorders – such as cases of aphasia, for instance (1945, 231–232) – in order to unveil and better understand the workings of language and perception in general because, as he explains, those particular cases are latent in all of us: "Whatever one's view of the relation between healthy and pathological behavior, speech must, in its normal functioning, be of such nature that disorders in it are always possible" (1973, 17). It is as if the dysfunctions and idiosyncrasies reveal the key to the workings of language which would ordinarily be hidden under the blanket of normality and habit.

And so just as Lecercle tries to uncover the workings of language through nonsensical texts and *the delirium of logophiliacs or mental patients*, so Merleau-Ponty, in his later work, explains the workings of language and expression through some of its most complex manifestations: literary texts and poetry. For instance in *La Prose du Monde* (1969), he engages with the work of Stendhal and Paul Valéry and justifies his choice by explaining that "the phenomenon of expression belongs both to the scientific study of language and to that of literary experience, and that these two studies overlap" (1973, 15). So looking at multilingual poetry will hopefully reveal some of the workings of multilingual and bilingual expression, but when searching for a suitable piece of nonsensical poetry by Bergvall, I had more difficulties than anticipated. Bergvall's work is not of the traditional *nonsensical* kind, it does not belong to what Lecercle defines as the canon of nonsensical literature, yet it pays particular attention to the many meanings of words. I eventually settled for a piece Bergvall presented at London College of Communication which challenged my own understanding of the meaning of words. The piece was part of an installation titled "Say Parsley" (2010). It takes its title from a brutal massacre in the Dominican Republic in 1937 during which Creole Haitians were murdered for not pronouncing 'parsley' (*perejil*) in the appropriate Spanish pronunciation by rolling the "R." In her presentation, words were projected on the wall and spoken in different languages; starting with 'parsley,' the words eventually lost their meaning altogether. All I could hear were sounds. I could not understand the language they were uttered in so it seemed 'normal' after all to lose track and hear only sounds, devoid of meaning. But now and again I could almost hear 'parsley,' then the French *persil*, and meaning reappeared. The piece has a very tragic implication: it is about language used as a justification to kill. But it is also a work about the transience of meaning, with the succession of languages at times hiding and at times revealing the meaning of the word to the listener depending on the language it is uttered in.

Bergvall's three letter word 'cat' in "Cat in the Throat" conjured up another three letter example where I seemed to be able to *drift in and out of meaning*. If I read the letters C.A.R., which happen to form the first syllable of my first name, those three letters, without the rest of my name, do not mean anything. Lecercle would say in a linguistic analysis that they have no semantic value. But by *car*, you will recognise, depending on the language you inhabit, either as a private motorised vehicle, 'a car' in English, or a coach, '*un car*,' in French. And when you think about it a little more you'll find that it is also a connective word in French, meaning 'because.' Now from this very simple example I would like to draw two main lines of thought. The first relates to phenomenology and stems from the idea that one needs to inhabit a language in order to *make sense* of it. The other relates to the absence of meaning and the space in-between.

First, let us start from the hypothesis that, as Merleau-Ponty (1945, 228) and Adrian Forty (2000, 15–16) declare, one can only inhabit one language at a time and that words take their meaning from the language in which they are uttered. In this case, in order to make sense of the word, one needs to make an active choice as to which language to read the word *car* in. Although I have some reservations about such a simplification, which I will develop later, let us consider that the meaning of the word *car* does indeed come from the 'positioning' of the reader into one linguistic world or the other, in this case English, or French. To make sense of a word in a different language requires the active participation of the reader, an effort of translation into one or another *langue* in order to have access to meaning. This creates a space, an in-between, which is in constant flux between languages, and where the bilingual subject oscillates between meanings. '*To mean*,' or what Lecercle also refers to as '*vouloir dire*,' (1994, 17) needs to be intentional. For the bilingual subject, the decision is accompanied by a 'positioning' within one or the other language.

The second point I want to make about the CAR example is that the speaker could, like Italo Calvino's character in *If on a winter's night a traveller*, decide to 'unlearn' both languages (1998, 49) and see CAR as a group of letters, devoid of meaning. The reader could decide not to assign any particular meaning to the letters. If we have seen that the space between languages is one of oscillation towards one or the other meaning, it is also possible to intentionally suspend meaning and remain in the middle.

In *Philosophy of Nonsense* (1994), Lecercle offers a reading of the literature of nonsense that will help us refine the analysis on the absence of meaning. He explains that if the very name of the genre seems to point at the absence of meaning in the text, it isn't so, and that "Writing outside sense proves to be surprisingly difficult, for meaning puts up a fight"(1994, 115). Nonsensical texts, by denying meaning, in fact, betray our fascination and need for meaning. Looking at the canons of nonsense literature and the work of Lewis Carroll, Lecercle refers to the Mad Hatter's riddle in *Alice's Adventures in Wonderland* – "why is the raven like a writing-desk?" – and explains that "both speakers [the Hatter and Lewis Carroll] do not want to know what it means – they want it not to mean, what they mean is not to mean" (1994, 118). While this citation suggests that there exists a space where meaning is suspended, Lecercle explains that for him:

> There is no *dire* without its *vouloir dire*. When he seems not to mean anything, the author of nonsense intends that it should be so: he has taken care of the sense, or rather of the non-sense, and the nonsense sounds take care of themselves.
>
> (1994, 127)

For Lecercle, literature of nonsense cannot escape meaning, for it is precisely what it seeks to hide. But this remark comes under the heading 'Meaning and Saying' and assumes that what we say, we mean. Our use of language is motivated, and its meaning can sometimes reach beyond what we intended it to be. An analysis under the heading 'Meaning and Listening,' however, might yield a different conclusion. The meaning of a text only materialises when we reach or inhabit the language of its author. However, one can hear, or read, without making sense, as is the case, for instance, when hearing or reading in a totally foreign language.

If the literature of nonsense offers a reflection on meaning and is open to interpretations and oscillations, 'non-sense,' by comparison, is the (relatively) static space of in-between. It is where no sense is made, where the reader cannot or does not want to inhabit one *langue* or another and the entire body participates in that refusal or inability to make sense. In 'non-sense,' hyphenation, like a pause or a *respiration* and separation, marks a difference from Lecercle's nonsense, and the *non* effectively stands for a negation, an abstention. This is the space where one makes no effort to make sense, or refuses to do so, instead preferring to remain between one and the other *langue*.

Bergvall's poem "Crop" oscillates between three languages. Each stanza is made of a first line in English, a second in Norwegian and a third in French. The poem might appear at first as a series of translations from one language to the next, but as the reader progresses it becomes obvious that the relationship between the three languages is of a different nature. The structure of the poem, juxtaposing the three languages, does less to reinforce the proximity and similarities of the chosen languages, than to highlight the space between the languages and their differences:

> Some thought they had their body safely then were asked to leave it behind the door or parts of it

som trodde at de trygt hadde sin kropp bare for å bli bedt om
å la den bli igjen bak døren eller deler av den
ceux dont le corps emporté au loin des leurs

Some hoped they had one safely only to find it had to be left
across the border or parts of it
som håpet de trygt hadde en kropp bare for å innse at den
måtte bli igjen over grensen eller deler av den
ceux dont le corps à la frontière nié n'est pas des leurs
     (2011, 149. Font colour changes appear in the original)

The repetitions and differences from one stanza to the next give the poem a sense of gradual evolution by calling for direct comparisons between consecutive stanzas. Yet when I read the poem, some lines are lost on me. I make sense of the English and the French, but not the Norwegian unfortunately. What Bergvall shows us in that poem is that in the transit between languages, parts of the body are lost, just as some of the words are dropped or truncated in the unfolding of her poem. The poem begins with a short paragraph in English, referring to her personal experience. At a point in her life when she decides, as a multilingual writer, to live and work mostly *in* the English language, Bergvall asks herself, rather anxiously perhaps, whether it is possible to retain the integrity of one's own body in the transit from one language to another:

> How does one keep ones body as ones own, what does this mean but the relative safety of boundaries, could I make sure that what I call my body would remain in the transit from othr languages, that it would hold its progression into English [...]
> (2011, 147)

In this introductory paragraph words are cropped, sometimes violently so, and letters – such as the 'e' in 'other' – are missing. In the following lines of the poem limbs or entire bodies are amputated in the crossing of boundaries, reminding us of the violence exerted onto the Haitians having to pronounce the word 'parsley.' Or, perhaps, words are lost more inconspicuously when one can no longer speak his or her native tongue in a country of adoption. During the transit from one language to another, not only do words get "bent, broken or lost along the way" (Evans 1997, 154) but so does the body: "Some thought they had their body safely then were asked to leave it behind the door or parts of it." In the first part of the poem the emphasis is on the violent loss of the body, of body parts, exerted by others, under pressure, where desire is taken away and the body separated against one's will from those it belongs with (*les leurs*). We notice, of course, that languages are being handled roughly all the same, as they reflect the brutality of the bodily experience. Words and letters in the first paragraph are dropped – violently – irrespective of the rules of grammar or orthography, and the juxtaposition of the three languages itself generates consecutive slippages.

Then there's a cut. A discontinuity in the poem. Two isolated lines in English, halfway through the text, break the regular structure of the poem:

> Some bodies are forgotten in the language compounds
> Some immense pressure is applied on to the forgetting of the ecosystems some escape from
> (2011, 150)

There is no Norwegian response to these lines, no French response either. The poem resumes its progression in three languages, but a subtle shift has taken place. In the next stanza, the bodies have been dropped and the French line reads: "*disparaissent comme les langues*," "Disappear like languages." The second part of the poem could be seen as a litany on the disappearance of language, "Some or many disappear," yet might still apply to the disappearance of bodies. In fact, it is both. *Words are body*, they become part of us, they induce certain feelings, sensations, meanings we can sense, hence the feeling of loss of part of the body as we lose the words. In *Phénoménologie de la perception*, Merleau-Ponty explains how we incorporate words, how they become part of us and how we use them, just as we would any other part of our expressive body. He writes:

> Il faut dire de l'image verbale ce que nous disions plus haut de la "représentation du mouvement": je n'ai pas besoin de me représenter l'espace extérieur et mon propre corps pour mouvoir l'un dans l'autre. Il suffit qu'ils existent pour moi et qu'ils constituent un certain champ d'action tendu autour de moi. De la même manière, je n'ai pas besoin de me représenter le mot pour le savoir et pour le prononcer. Il suffit que j'en possède l'essence articulaire et sonore comme l'une des modulations, l'un des usages possibles de mon corps.
> (1945, 220)

> We must say of the verbal image what we said above of the "representation of movement": I have no need of representing to myself external space and my own body in order to move the one within the other. It is enough that they exist for me and that they constitute a certain field of action held around me. Likewise, I have no need of representing to myself the word in order to know it and to pronounce it. It is enough that I possess its articulatory and sonorous essence as one of the modulations or one of the possible uses of my body.[2]
>
> (2012, 186)

The lungs, the tongue, the cheeks are all involved in our expressive endeavour, but we do not represent the movements of all those parts of the body when we say something, we just say the words. We do not need to refer to the definition of the words either, or even the different encounters we have had with them in order to say them. Words produce a certain feeling, a number of sensations, which the body, in turn, will register and incorporate. From this point onwards words become part of what Merleau-Ponty calls our 'equipment,' they become integral part of our speaking body. In her poem Bergvall starts by asking herself "how [she] could make sure that what [she] calls [her] body would remain in the transit from othr languages," she then shows that in the transit from one language to another, parts of the speaking body, some of its modulations, are lost. What matters here is the consideration of the corporeity of words and the understanding of what happens when political pressure is applied, in the crossing of border, so that some words can no longer be spoken as in Bergvall's poem. Merleau-Ponty explains the uniqueness of words, the specificity of these articulations or modulations of the body and how one word cannot simply be replaced by another word in another language:

> La prédominance des voyelles dans une langue, des consonnes dans une autre, les systèmes de construction et de syntaxe ne représenteraient pas autant de conventions arbitraires pour exprimer la même pensée, mais plusieurs manières pour le corps humain de célébrer le monde et finalement de le vivre. De là viendrait que le sens *plein* d'une langue n'est jamais traduisible dans une autre.
>
> (1945, 228)

The predominance of vowels in one language, of consonants in another, or systems of construction and syntax would not represent so many arbitrary conventions for expressing the same thought, but rather several ways for the human body to celebrate the world and to finally live it. This is why the *full* sense of a language is never translatable into another.

(2012, 193)

So when a speaking subject is no longer allowed to use a particular language or *langue* it has learnt and incorporated, the body suffers a loss and as Bergvall writes "Some bodies like languages are lost." Translation studies have many times over addressed the question of untranslatability in debates which focus on faithfulness to the original text, the recourse to a third text or notion of non-equivalence. It is this notion that interests us here. Not on a purely semantic level as is generally considered in linguistic studies, but rather at the level of language embodiment. There is no bodily equivalence between words of different languages and as Bergvall shows in her poem, the migrant speaker "leaves behind the door" or "behind the border" some sensations that cannot be replicated in the other language.

Words are *unique* modulations of our being. But although they will not be expressed or exteriorised anymore, I would argue that those words still exist, inside the body, and the modulations remain a possibility. So the loss might not be as total as it first appeared. As Bergvall's poem progresses, the words 'disappear' and '*disparaissent*' are replaced by 'arise' and '*se lèvent*.' This choice of words finally gives hope as they evoke the sunrise (*le soleil se lève* in French) while also relating to the body – rising up in the morning (se lever). The words used by Bergvall evoke the rebirth of the speaking body and when she writes that "Some that arise in some of us arrive in each of us," language it seems, new languages, other languages, become available again to the body. Bergvall no longer speaks of 'language compounds' or 'ecosystems,' like forces that are external to us, but clearly of something internal to the body, emerging from within "in some of us," "in each of us." A sense of community is also present in these last lines with the pronoun 'us,' and language is shared collectively. At the end of the poem, language prevails, and the body, previously torn and cropped, remains host to many (some) languages and finds its unity again in a sense of shared community. If the body is not whole in one language only, its integrity can be found in the multiplicity of languages.

In Bergvall's poem, three languages are present and three voices emerge from Bergvall's body. Yet if they each have their own way to celebrate the world, with the different phonic and grammatical differences Merleau-Ponty refers to, it is clear in this poem that the voices are not separate. They might be distinct, but they are not separate. The Norwegian line reads like an echo to the English line and the French line like an echo to the Norwegian line, yet the Norwegian line is not a translation from the English one, nor is the French line a translation from the Norwegian in the narrow sense of the term. Instead, each line forms what is almost a response to the previous one and a discursive relation is in place between the three languages. The three languages talk to each other. Inside her. And so Bergvall's body is made of all these modulations, either latent, or expressed. Only some might be more difficult or require more effort to recall and to reactivate.

Notes

1 An earlier version of this essay was delivered on 19 September 2014 at the *Art in Translation* Biennale organised by the University of Iceland at the Nordic House in Reykjavik. The theme of the biennale was "The Art of Being in Between." In this essay, every effort has been made to retain the immediacy of the spoken word.
2 The *essence articulaire et sonore*, translated as "articulatory and sonorous essence" by Donald A. Landes, is a strange contorted wording to say the least, rendered even stranger through translation. Colin Smith's choice of the words "articulatory and acoustic style" in his translation is also uneasy. It reminds us nevertheless of Saussure's analysis of what he calls *l'appareil vocal* (1916, 67), where he explains phonics in great detail, listing all the organs involved in the forming of sounds. *Expiration, articulation buccale* are absolutely necessary, he says, and might be complemented by *vibration du larynx* and *résonance nasale*.

Works Cited

Bergvall, Caroline. 2010. *Say Parsley.* Arnolfini Gallery.
———. 2011. *Meddle English.* New York: Nightboat Books.
Calvino, Italo. 1998. *If on a Winter's Night a Traveller*, translated by William Weaver. London: Vintage.
Cixous, Hélène. 1993. *Three Steps on the Ladder of Writing*, translated by Sarah Cornell and Susan Sellers. New York: Columbia University Press.
Derrida, Jacques. 1972. *Marges de la Philosophie.* Paris: Editions de Minuit.
Evans, Robin. 1997. *Translations from Drawing to Building and Other Essays.* London: Janet Evans and Architectural Association Publications.
Forty, Adrian. 2000. *Words and Buildings: A Vocabulary of Modern Architecture.* London: Thames & Hudson.
Lecercle, Jean-Jacques. 1990. *The Violence of Language.* London: Routledge.
———. 1994. *Philosophy of Nonsense.* London: Routledge.

Merleau-Ponty, Maurice. 1945. *Phénoménologie de la perception*. Paris: Gallimard.
———. 1969. "La Science et l'expérience de l'expression" in *La Prose du Monde*. Paris: Gallimard.
———. 1973. *The Prose of the World*, translated by John O'Neill. Evanston: Northwest University Press.
———. 2012. *Phenomenology of Perception*, translated by Donald A. Landes. Oxon: Routledge.
Saussure, Ferdinand de. 1916. *Cours de linguistique générale*. Paris: Payot.

5   Louis Wolfson's Reformed Body[1]

I shall speak of an American writer who writes in my mother tongue.
I shall speak in the American writer's own mother tongue, though it is not my own.
He would not hear this. These words would hurt him.

Louis Wolfson is an American who writes in French, but an odd and peculiar kind of French, where the struggle of language can be heard. A language learnt in textbooks in the confines of his study. A language learnt by a violated body.

From the title of his book, Wolfson (1970) refers to himself at once as *'schizo,' 'psychotique'* and *'étudiant de langues schizophrénique.'* Having suffered all kinds of horrific treatments in psychiatric hospitals, Wolfson identifies his mother as the person who facilitated these torturous experiences by committing him to mental institutions. She becomes for him a source of immense pain. Under her care, however, and unable to provide for himself, he has no choice but to endure her presence. This situation is for him extremely distressing: he cannot physically bear the sound of his mother's high-pitched voice, and by extension, every word uttered or read in English hurts him just the same. In order to escape his mother tongue, he embarks on the simultaneous study of four foreign languages: French, German, Hebrew and Russian. Thus armed with new-found knowledge, various bodily contraptions and an implacable and unfailing reasoning ability, he undertakes to kill his mother tongue.

Despite his precautions to avoid the English language, he sometimes happens to hear or read English words, either accidentally or forcefully. On encountering those words, he manages to alleviate his pain by way of complex literary transformations, using a system of instantaneous homophonic translation. Not content with replacing the hurtful English words by foreign words of similar meaning,

Wolfson looks for words of similar sound, so that what he hears becomes for him, quasi-instantaneously, a foreign language:

> En effet, ayant un mot étranger remplissant, à la fois dans le son et dans le sens, les conditions, selon lui, de similitude avec un mot anglais donné, celui-ci ne lui semblait plus guère exister, et l'écouter, ce lui serait plus ou moins écouter le mot étranger similaire. Et, à ces moments, il avait, mais peut-être à tord, l'espérance de pouvoir un jour à nouveau employer normalement sa langue maternelle, dont usaient presque exclusivement les gens qui l'entouraient.
>
> (1970, 63)

> Indeed, having found a foreign word fulfilling, according to him, both by sound and meaning, the criteria of similarity with a given English word, the latter seemed to have disappeared, and hearing it would be, more or less, like hearing the similar foreign word. In those moments, he hoped, perhaps wrongly, that he might one day use again his mother tongue, which people around him used almost exclusively.
>
> (translation my own)

The similitude of sound turns what would otherwise have been categorised as a simple translation into a different experience where one language is instantaneously replaced by another. 'Vegetable oil,' he explains, can easily be heard as the German *vegetabilisches Ol*.

Wolfson writes of his linguistic knowledge as a 'linguistic weapon' (1970, 62). Here we are witnessing a battle, and despite Wolfson's having learnt four languages, it sometimes proves difficult to find any single suitable word to replace the English word. In such cases, Wolfson undertakes a precise yet violent operation, slicing up all undesirable words phonetically in order to recompose them using a combination of words from different languages. He uses language as a weapon, and Saussurean linguistics as a sword, in order to dismantle his mother tongue. He decomposes each word into a series of phonemes,[2] which he then turns into a foreign word or foreign phoneme. Wolfson has an obsessive attitude to food consumption and pays particular attention to food labels, so, for example, in 'shortening' (in reference to 'vegetable shortening' found on some food packagings), the sound *sh* becomes the Hebrew *chèmenn*, meaning 'oil' or 'fat,' or might even become the German *Schmalz*, meaning 'melted fat,' the sound *r*, coupled with *ch* again, becomes the Russian *jir*, meaning 'fat' and 'lard,' and finally the suffix *-ing* becomes the German *-ung* (53–56). The transformations are rather technical, they follow complex semantic and phonological paths, and, in this case, they do not result in a particular word, but rather an assemblage of sounds from different languages which Wolfson hears successively. Wolfson also transforms full sentences: "Do you want a pad," for example, becomes, three pages later, "*tu' taboyou wünshst achad padoùchka*" (164–167) (here the words are kept whole but borrowed from different languages: German, Russian, German, Hebrew, Russian) or "don't trip over the wire" becomes "*nicht trébucher über èt Zwirn*" (German, French, German, Hebrew, German) (205–212). These operations, the dismantling and reconstructing of words, which Wolfson himself qualifies as "bizarre, artificial, against nature but obviously acceptable and even necessary" (62, translation my own), alleviate his pain and give him satisfaction. The world he creates as the result of his rejection of the English language is multilingual and entirely his own. Wolfson inhabits a linguistic world which bears no trace of his painful English experience, but instead belongs to mute dictionaries and linguists' textbooks. He refrains, however, from using etymological dictionaries, which might contain English words, and he also avoids all bilingual dictionaries containing the English language.

In his essay "Wolfson & Sons," François Cusset (2009) remarks that Wolfson has a "*patronyme freudien prédestiné*," or is aptly named: Wolfson is 'wolf's son,' the son of a wild animal feared by man and ostracised. The word *son* in French also means 'sound.' Cusset's title is a direct reference to both the legacy of Wolfson's work and his use of sounds. Louis, it is worth noting here, also bears an uncanny phonetic resemblance to the French word *l'ouïe*, meaning 'sense of hearing,' and of course there's also a lineage of French Kings named Louis. Louis, from Old French *Loois*, means 'famous in war.'[3] Coincidence it might be, striking nonetheless.

Wolfson is at war with the English language. In the same essay Cusset writes that Wolfson's system of transformations – his "small device, artisan virus or army knife" (152 translation my own) – enables him to defeat the entire Empire of the Sign. Wolfson, he adds, is the embodiment or perhaps even the resolution of a debate dating back to Nietzsche and Mallarmé: a debate about "the materiality of language, the obsession of a language which does not represent or signifies anymore, but *is*, a language which does not designate or replace, but *does*" (151–152 translation my own).

Wolfson, I would argue, does not so much end the hegemony of the sign but, rather, brings the reader's attention to the sign in order to shift the reader's attention to his or her senses. He achieves this through descriptions of his own extreme bodily sensations while overeating for instance or during his regular colonic irrigations. I note here that his descriptions, and indeed the entire book, are written in the third person, thus placing the narrator at a certain distance from his own experience. But in a way, the third person, which appears to separate Wolfson *the narrator* from Wolfson *the main character*, also has the effect of bringing the narrator and the reader closer together by placing them both in the position of observers. Wolfson and the reader share a similar perspective on the main protagonist's adventures, which seems to add to the lucidity of the text.

We have seen how Wolfson fights with an excess of reason and an almost scientific method to dismantle and annihilate the English words. He also uses shields to protect his fragile body. And, indeed, the book that interested so many writers, linguists, philosophers and psychoanalysts for its extraordinary contribution to language, starts, not with complex literary transformations, but with a description of his own body. The book opens with the following paragraph:

> Le jeune homme schizophrénique était maigre comme beaucoup de gens dans de tels état mentaux. En effet, il semblait plutôt mal nourri. Peut-être était-il même dans un état de marasme ; du moins sa mère semblait-elle quelquefois penser ceci. Les os malaires du jeune homme faisaient saillie nettement, les joues étaient creuses et les veines étaient bien distinctes à travers la peau mince. En conséquence de sa vie très sédentaire, presque celle d'un invalide (ce qu'il était de plusieurs points de vue), il avait très peu de musculature et était très faible, cette faiblesse étant peut-être un important facteur de la grande peur que reflétaient ses yeux grands ouverts: peur de la nature ainsi que de ses semblables, peur de la mort aussi bien, en quelque sorte, que de la vie. Son visage et en particulier sa bouche semblaient le plus souvent grimacés par un mélange de tristesse et de douleur, la bouche étant du reste plutôt petite et les commissures des lèvres dirigées en bas.
>
> (1970, 29)

The schizophrenic young man was skinny, like many people in such mental states. Indeed, he seemed rather malnourished. Perhaps was he even in the doldrums; at least his mother seemed to think so sometimes. The young man's jawbones were clearly pointing out, his cheeks were hollow and his veins distinctly visible through his thin skin. As a consequence of his sedentary life, almost the life of a disabled person (which he was on various accounts), he had very little muscle and was very weak; this weakness perhaps was an important factor of the great fear reflected in his wide open eyes: fear of nature as well as his peers, fear of death, as well as, to some extent, life. His face, and in particular his mouth seemed most of the time to be grimacing in a combination of sadness and pain, his mouth being in fact rather small and the corner of his lips pointing downwards.

(translation my own)

Wolfson's weak nature seems at odds with the energy and effort he deploys in order to constantly protect himself from the intrusive English-speaking world around him. He uses his fingers to protect his eardrums from his mother's verbal assaults. He also uses sound, the sound of his own vocal chords to cover his mother's voice:

> "Je ne sais pas," répondit-il morose en allemand et tout en enfonçant plus profond dans les oreilles les bouts des pouces, les coudes sur les marges externes d'un grand, épais dictionnaire médical en un volume en langue étrangère, ouvert vers le milieu et qu'il employait habituellement comme un accoudoir en lisant quelque livre placé là-dessus, les poings à ce moment-là à demi fermés et le dos des quatres doigts (au niveau de la partie distale de la première phalange) appuyé contre l'os malaire de chaque côté et les jointures des doigts contre les tempes, et tout en faisant des bruits continus simultanément par un mouvement oscillatoire des pouces contre la surface intérieure des conduits auditifs et par des vibrations des cordes vocales, et tout pour ne plus écouter les propos de maman.
>
> (1970, 66–67)

> "I don't know," he replies, morose, in German, all the while pushing the end of his thumbs deeper into his ears, his elbows on the margins of a large, thick medical dictionary in one volume in a foreign language, opened towards the middle, and which he habitually used as an armrest whilst reading some book placed atop, his fists at the time half clenched and the back of his four fingers (at the distal part of the first phalanx) resting against the jaw bone on either side and the fingers joints against his temples, all the while making simultaneous continuous noises with an oscillating movement of his thumbs against the interior surface

of his ear ducts and vibrations of his vocal chords, all in order to stop listening to mum's words.

(translation my own)

He also resorts to contraptions such as the headphones of his portable transistor, which he carries around with a set of spare batteries. He tunes onto the local Hispanic radio as well as programmes from Cologne, Moscow and Paris. He also protects his eyes from the onslaught of English words and regularly keeps either a foreign language book or dictionary open in front of him. He even uses these as backgrounds or props to other books he reads. He kills the English language with an excess of other languages.

Wolfson also suffers from extreme food behaviour. At times starving himself and, at others, succumbing to eating excesses. The sensory experiences described at length and with extreme precision are often associated with his customary, nonetheless extraordinary, linguistic gymnastics:

> Donc, il répétait les mêmes quatre ou cinq mots vingt ou trente fois tandis qu'il ingérait avec avidité un montant de calories égal en milliers à la première partie de numéros, se farcissant la bouche de gros morceaux de nourriture, de petits gâteaux et de biscuits tout entiers, et tout en frottant plus ou moins fortement les aliments contre les lèvres non récemment lavées et donc peut-être portant des œufs ou même des larves de vers parasites [...]
>
> (1970, 49)

> While repeating the same four or five words twenty or thirty times, he absorbed an amount of calories equal in thousands to the first figures, stuffing his mouth with large pieces of food, cakes and whole biscuits, whilst rubbing the food with more or less pressure against his lips, which had not been recently washed and thus might carry eggs or larva of parasitic worms [...]
>
> (translation my own)

The binge could last two hours or more, it would last beyond hunger, beyond him feeling pain in his stomach. Wolfson indulges in an excess of sensations. We have seen earlier that he was able to assimilate the words 'vegetable oil' as the German *vegetabilisches Ol*, but his interest in vegetable oil is not only linguistic. He has read in a medical journal that vegetable oil was better for the body than animal fat and proceeds to fill his body with as much vegetable oil as possible.

Through eating and the sensations it procures him, he assimilates not only the food, but the German words as well: he creates bodily sensations which he can associate with the words otherwise devoid of physical experience. These words, we have seen, were initially learnt in textbooks and thus dissociated from any bodily sensations or rather could only be associated with his 'learning' posture, sat in his study, his elbows on his desk and fingers in his ears. Food enables him to feel the words differently.

> Car le langage, l'expérience du jeune homme schizophrénique nous l'indique, est avant tout une prouesse physique, une capacité d'absorption, de digestion.
>
> (Le Clézio 2009, 46)
>
> Because language, as the experience of the schizophrenic young man shows, is above all a physical feat, a capacity of absorption, of digestion.
>
> (translation my own)

Wolfson's lengthy description of colonic irrigations, which he sees as pleasurable experiences administered by women and compares to sexual experiences, are yet another manifestation of his search for excesses of sensations. His eating excesses are accompanied by purges. But what Wolfson purges himself of is not only toxins or food: he purges himself of specific words and their associated sensations. He relieves his body of any painful experiences associated with the English language before creating new extreme sensations associated with new foreign words during his binge eating sessions. He has not killed his mother, he has killed his own English-speaking body and erased all traces of bodily sensations the English language might have left on him. In his essay on Wolfson titled "La Tour de Babil" and quoted above, J.M.G Le Clézio explains that:

> Ce qui nous attire avec tant de vertige dans le livre de Wolfson, c'est ce qu'il évoque un drame que nous connaissons bien, et que nous avons voulu oublier: le drame du passage du langage.
>
> Nous avions voulu l'oublier: c'est que le monde du langage est un monde total, totalement fermé; il n'admet aucun compromis, aucun partage. Dès l'instant que nous y avons pénétré, il ne nous est plus possible de retourner en arrière – vers cet autre monde, celui du silence.
>
> (2009, 41)

What draws us with such dizzying force in Wolfson's book, is that he evokes a very familiar drama, a drama we have deliberately forgotten: the drama of the passage of language.

We wished to forget: because the world of language is total, totally closed; it tolerates no compromise, no division [*partage*]. As soon as we have entered it, it becomes impossible to turn back – towards this other world, the world of silence.

(translation my own)

Wolfson returns to the world of silence. With the colonic irrigations, his aim is to erase all traces of the English language and return to a pre-linguistic state before being able to express himself again. Once he is satisfied that his English body has been destroyed and disposed of, only then can he start and learn to express himself again. But if the practice of instantaneous translation into four different languages was used when hearing or reading existing English words, it was only used to *kill* the English language and not as a way to express himself. When Wolfson finally decides to express himself, he chooses not to write in the combination of languages he has learnt but instead decides on a single one: the French language. Wolfson starts the reconstruction of his speaking body in French. Le Clézio notes that this language, as well as the others he has learnt, is for Wolfson a dead language:

> Des langues mortes: ces langues sont parlées par des millions d'hommes, mais pour le jeune homme malade elles n'ont aucune réalité que cette réalité livresque, ou à la rigueur radiophonique. Il apprend avec surprise que le français est parlé par 75% de la population à Montréal – mais il n'est pas convaincu.

(2009, 47)

> Dead languages: languages spoken by millions of people, however for the young demented [*malade*] man, these languages have only a reality in books or possibly on the radio. He learns with surprise that the French language is spoken by 75% of the population in Montréal – but he is not convinced.

(translation my own)

This citation suggests that Wolfson only engaged with languages that bore no relation for him with other speakers. In her essay "Le sens perdu (ou le 'Schizo' et la signification)," psychiatrist and psychoanalyst Piera Aulagnier explains with great clarity how language is invested with a link to the person we learn it from and talks about the 'investissement libidinal' with the mother or 'libidinal involvement.' Given his relationship with his mother and his mother tongue, it seems therefore essential for Wolfson to learn languages which are in no way invested with a personal link to another speaker. We have seen how he learnt languages with textbooks, dictionaries and audio recordings but did not attend any language classes, for instance. Yet, Wolfson knew that nearly 80% people spoke French in Montréal; he had heard the figure on Radio-Canada (1970, 100) and even reveals having taken part in a writing competition organised by the radio – he reproduces in his book the 1,000 word competition entry, written in French (1970, 101–104). Wolfson knew that the French language was alive and intended to use it. But why did he decide to write his book in French I wonder and not any of the other languages he had learnt?

Might Radio-Canada's writing competition have been the incentive for Wolfson to write in French? The competition took place in 1967, for the *Exposition Universelle* of that year, in other words after the completion of Wolfson's first manuscript, which was sent to Gallimard in 1964, so this proposition ought to be excluded.

Was it because Saussure's *Cours de linguisitique générale* – which provided him with the necessary linguistic tools to dismantle the English words – are themselves written in French?

Was it because of his brief encounter with French-speaking workers, during which he was able to practise his newly found language?

Was it because of his forename, *Louis*, that he sought an affinity?

Was it because of Gallimard, to whom he entrusted his first book manuscript?

Was it because of the Oulipo group and Raymond Queneau who read the manuscript and saw in it a value that everyone else doubted?[4]

Was it because of certain words similarities, amongst them the 'library', compared at times to a prison (Wolfson 1970, 163), yet still a safe and quiet haven in which the schizophrenic student was able to take refuge?

Or was it because of the word '*malade*' that Wolfson took to replace the word 'mad'?

Wolfson does not disclose to the reader why he chose French to write his book. What appears, however, is that in order to make sense and recompose his body, the choosing of a single language provided him with a sense of unity, a sense of purpose, and even, a place to go to – as he intends to publish his book in France. The writing of his book, the necessary book, as Paul Auster pointed out (1975), is an attempt to create a new body from a pre-linguistic state. And in his effort, Wolfson chose the French language to express himself instead of oscillating across four languages as he had done so far. He aimed to communicate again, in a single language. And since the book is *autobiographical*, it creates along the way, new memories in French. Wolfson allows himself to relive his life in French and his life experiences have now, with the writing of the book, taken place in French.

His moving into the French language, however, was not a process of translation in the common sense of the word. Wolfson does not move from one linguistic world to another since he has carefully erased all traces, which might lead him back to the source language of his mother. He obliterated the source language. His method, instead, might be best compared to Jacques Derrida's concept of Absolute Translation, from a language which does not exist, or in Wolfson's case, has ceased to exist, to another language. In *Le Monolinguisme de l'autre*, Derrida (1996), speaks of the 'Otherness of Language.' The language that he speaks, he explains, his own language, the French language, is not his own but that of others. Derrida grew up in Algiers before moving to Paris to study philosophy. He talks of the alienation of the speaking subject, his dependence on others, on another culture, in his mode of expression and the hope, one day, to recover the language that was taken away from him at birth. Here, alienation and the sense of dependence are, of course, familiar words to the schizophrenic subject. In Wolfson's case, English, his mother tongue, was the alienating language, the language of his mother and his peers, the language of others around him. For Wolfson the French language, however, does not represent alienation, but liberation and expression. One might argue that by resorting to French, Wolfson suffers another kind of alienation. But if he has chosen to express himself in the French language, his text appears to retain an incredible freedom *from* the French language. If he has subdued himself to others again, it is only to books and libraries – as well as, to some extent, radio programmes – but not directly to living bodies. Finally, and most importantly, his desire to make sense, he explains, itself justifies his recourse to the French language:

> Quoi qu'il en soit, son incantation d'"optimiste" la plus récente est plutôt comme suit: sans doute une certaine sorte d'effort est-il nécessaire pour ne pas s'affaisser, pour ne pas s'arrêter, pour

continuer d'agir, pour "vivre", pour être "sensé", "lucide"..., peut-être bien qu'il s'y trouve une certaine difficulté même; mais peut-être faire cela est-ce, néanmoins, moins difficile – quelque paradoxal que ceci semble et même malgré un certain sentiment éventuel de scepticisme, d'incroyance, même de répugnance là-dessus au moment d'agir – que de s'affaisser, de s'arrêter, de tomber dans un état de stupeur...!
(1970, 255)

In any case, his most recent incantation as an "optimist" goes more like this: no doubt a certain sort of effort is necessary so as not to collapse, so as not to stop, so as to continue to act, so as to "live", so as to make "sense", to be "lucid"..., perhaps is there even a degree of difficulty there; but to do this might, nonetheless, be less difficult – as paradoxical as it seems and even despite a certain potential feeling of skepticism, of disbelief, of loathing even at the time of action – than to collapse, to stop, to fall into a state of stupor...!
(translation my own)

Wolfson here writes about the necessary physical effort required to make sense. In the absence of effort, Wolfson fears the collapse into the non-sensical, the absence of sense and the madness he has experienced before. In the same paragraph, he juxtaposes 'life' with 'making sense' and 'being lucid.' Is life measured by our ability to be sensical? Can we only live when we make the effort to make sense? Does it mean to be dead (or demented) if one falls into the space of non-sense, a pre-linguistic state of silence?

Wolfson's book doesn't end there, and we know that Wolfson submitted several pages to Gallimard with what he called a 'reformed orthography' in the hope that the entire manuscript could be reworked. In these new texts words were 'perfected' by the author, following simple phonetic rules: some double letters omitted, silent ones deleted, all the while trying to minimise the disruption these changes might incur in the dictionary. Removing the letter u after a q for instance, would be less disruptive than turning the q into a k in the great order of the dictionary. The reform pushes things further, he writes, but not to the extreme. Gallimard rejected the reformed orthography on the grounds that it would alienate the French reader and that no one would read it. Yet, giving in to Wolfson's request, Gallimard eventually agreed to publish a few extracts with the reformed orthography at the end of the book. If I were to read the extracts out loud you probably would not hear any difference from the rest of the book, yet the reading of these orthographically reformed texts requires another kind of effort. This time the reading, despite the so-called desire for simplification of the French language, is in fact made more difficult for the French reader. It is, for the French reader, like reading a foreign language, and the alienation lies in the effort one needs to deploy to make sense of it. The letter '*e*' is used for 'and' instead of the usual '*et*.' Other words like '*tems*' and '*öme*' *that* don't exist in French, replace the words '*temps*' and '*homme*.' So Wolfson effectively asks the French reader to translate the word '*tems*' into '*temps*' and the word '*öme*' into '*homme*' in order to make sense of the text. Before introducing his 'perfectionnement orthographique,' Wolfson apologises in advance to the reader as if aware of the trouble he is about to cause.[5] The reading of Wolfson's reformed language requires the effort that Wolfson himself had to put into the writing of his 'French' version. It is like reading a translation from the French language into Wolfson's very own language and with this reformed text Wolfson invites the reader to experience his struggle with language. Here the reader needs to make an effort to make sense of the linguistic sign, or else remain in the space of non-sense. And this is Wolfson's revenge, his way of forcing the reader to make sense, just as he had been forced to. The effort the reader makes is the force required to free themselves from the alienation of language and finally make sense of the text.

Notes

1 This essay was first read at the American Comparative Literature Association (ACLA) annual conference on 19 March 2016 at Harvard University, in Cambridge, Massachusetts. It was presented as part of a panel proposed by Dominique Jullien, Mads Rosendahl Thomsen and Wen-Chin Ouyang on "Writing Between Worlds: Multilingualism as a Creative Force."
2 Acoustic units described by Ferdinand de Saussure in *Cours de linguistique générale* (1916, 63–66).
3 Etymonline. 2018. "Louis." Accessed July 2018. http://www.etymonline.com/word/louis
4 Note that Wolfson's second book is clearly Oulipien: *Ma mère, musicienne, est morte de maladie maligne à minuit, mardi à mercredi, au milieu du mois de mai mille977 au mouroir Memorial à Manhattan*. 2012. Editions Attila.
5 "Si l'auteur doit s'excuser d'avoir écrit et fait publier ce livre, il le fait séance tenante" (Wolfson 1970, 259).
    "Should the author apologize for having written and published this book, he does so forthwith" (translation my own).

Works Cited

Aulagnier, Piera. 2009. "Le Sens Perdu (ou le 'Schizo' et la signification)" in *Dossier Wolfson,* edited by Jean-Bertrand Pontalis, Jean-Marie Gustave Le Clézio, Paul Auster, Piera Aulagnier, Max Dorra, Michel Foucault, Pierre Alferi and François Cusset. Paris: Gallimard.

Auster, Paul. 1975. "One Man Language" in *The New York Review of Books* 6 February.

Le Clézio, J.M.G. 2009. "La Tour de Babil" in *Dossier Wolfson,* edited by Jean-Bertrand Pontalis, Jean-Marie Gustave Le Clézio, Paul Auster, Piera Aulagnier, Max Dorra, Michel Foucault, Pierre Alferi and François Cusset. Paris: Gallimard.

Cusset, François. 2009. "Wolfson & Sons" in *Dossier Wolfson,* edited by Jean-Bertrand Pontalis, Jean-Marie Gustave Le Clézio, Paul Auster, Piera Aulagnier, Max Dorra, Michel Foucault, Pierre Alferi and François Cusset. Paris: Gallimard.

Derrida, Jacques. 1996. *Le Monolinguisme de l'autre ou la prothèse d'origine.* Paris: Galillée.

Wolfson, Louis. 1970. *Le Schizo et les langues, ou la phonétique chez le psychotique (esquisses d'un étudiant de langues schizophrénique).* Paris: Gallimard.

———. [1984] 2012. *Ma mère, musicienne, est morte de maladie maligne à minuit, mardi à mercredi, au milieu du mois de mai mille977 au mouroir Memorial à Manhattan.* Editions Attila.

6 The Political Bilingual Body
One's Right to the Other Language[1]

I have chosen to write this essay in the French language. I write in French, yet we are in Italy. My previous presentations were all written in the English language and over the years I have written a number of *papers*. But since my last presentation, something has happened, a vote whereby millions and millions of small ballot papers have turned me into a foreign body, a foreigner in my adoptive country. This country I considered mine also, since it was European.

Today I will read two essays, one in French and the other in English. In other words, one in my mother tongue and the other in my adoptive or adopted tongue. The first text is the transcript of Jacques Derrida's seminar on Hospitality, delivered in Paris in 1996, whilst the second is the transcript of a lecture delivered by Lisa Robertson in Vancouver in 2010. Despite the 14 years that separates them, both texts operate in similar ways: they are both intended to university audiences and both texts are verbal *addresses*. We should also add that both were written, and spoken, by writers who interrogate the workings of language, whether through philosophy or through poetry.

Allow me today to proceed not chronologically, but starting with what constitutes the 'motive' force of this presentation: an extract from Lisa Robertson's essay – and to continue thereof by moving between both essays.

> Discourse improvises, unmoored to any stable geographic or architectural foundation. We citizens constitute ourselves according to the movement of subjectivity in language. At the same time, we are administratively identified by shared, conventional borders, and a historical concept of collective and individual rights or those rights' withdrawal.
>
> (2018, 2)

Published in Canada as "Untitled Essay," and forming part of the collection *Nilling* (2012), Robertson's essay was first presented during a conference on the theme "Citizenship and Domestic Space" at Simon Fraser University. It has recently been published again in London by Book Works and The Common Guild, at a very appropriate time, under the title "Thresholds: A Prosody of Citizenship." The essay has travelled across oceans as has Robertson who now lives in France.

In her essay, Robertson discusses the vernacular as a shared language learnt not simply from dictionaries and textbooks, but from a subject's collective experience or co-existence. She describes vernacular language as "something which loosely gathers whatever singular words and cadences move a given situation, a given meeting, as it is being lived by its speakers" (2018, 17). Robertson refers to Dante's essay "De vulgari eloquentia" in which vernacular language is the 'natural' language of children and their nurses (2018, 6). She also draws parallels between vernacular language and Michel Foucault's discourse (2018, 9, 16), but refutes any possible comparison between vernacular language and Ferdinand de Saussure's *langue*, arguing that Saussure's 'fixed' language fails to contend with a subjectivity in constant evolution (2018, 16). Yet we will see that comparisons and useful rapprochements can be made between Robertson's *Prosody of Citizenship* and Saussure's linguistics. For instance, Robertson's words cited above "Discourse improvises, unmoored to any stable geographic or architectural foundation," resonate with Saussure's claim that *langues* and dialects have no natural boundaries (1916, 275–278).

However, Robertson invites us to think language differently, beyond Saussure's structuralist approach, Foucault's discourse and Dante's vernacular. Borrowing from the linguist Emile Benveniste, and later from the works of poet and translator Henri Meschonnic, Robertson explains that language is not only a mode of expression or a tool of communication, but that language ultimately creates the speaking subject. Language gives rise to the political subject at the heart of society:

> As soon as she speaks and names, the political subject emerges. Her agency is a verbal one; architecture and governance can only interpret, fix or abstract the fluency of the linguistic given.
> (2018, 3)

As such, Robertson's definition can be said to differ from Foucault's *discours*, defined [*en creux*] by the boundaries of control systems and institutions which limit the speaking subject and sometimes suffocate it. Robertson, to the contrary, speaks of the birth of the subject through speech and adds:

> Co-citizens, in Benveniste's historicist linguistics, are those who speak together, and their home is the vulnerable shelter that speaking together offers them, for the duration of speech's intensity. Urban, architectural, sartorial and semiotic surfaces may receive, refract and carry the traces of such meetings, but cannot limit them. The space of the citizen is not bounded but semantically inflected.
>
> (2018, 11)

For Roberston there is no boundary between private and public, no threshold to cross between *Domus* and *Civis*, the domestic and the urban; instead vernacular language is a relational construction between individuals living together under the same roof or in the same country, and the difference between *Domus* and *Civis* would simply be a difference of scale. Robertson reminds us nonetheless that a citizen always exists within an administrative context:

> At the same time, we are administratively identified by shared, conventional borders, and a historical concept of collective and individual rights or those rights' withdrawal.
>
> (2018, 2)

At a time when some of our rights are effectively threatened, it becomes crucial to reassess the subjectivity of the speaking subject.

These rights are geo-localised indeed, circumscribed to a particular territory, and if language itself doesn't know any geographical boundary, the speaking subject on the other hand, or more precisely the speaking body as it is geo-localised in a particular country at a given moment, must abide by the official language of the law and therefore come up against linguistic boundaries. For Derrida, this constitutes one of the first shortfalls of the principle of hospitality. The laws of hospitality themselves, those meant to welcome foreigners into a country, are written in a language which they do not have access to:

> [...] l'étranger est d'abord étranger à la langue du droit dans laquelle est formulé le devoir d'hospitalité, le droit d'asile, ses limites, ses normes, sa police, etc. Il doit demander l'hospitalité dans une langue qui par définition n'est pas la sienne, celle que

> lui impose le seigneur, le pouvoir, la nation, l'Etat, le père, etc. Celui-ci lui impose la traduction dans sa propre langue, et c'est la première violence.
>
> (1997, 21)

> [...] the foreigner is first of all foreign to the legal language in which the duty of hospitality is formulated, the right to asylum, its limits, norms, policing, etc. he has to ask for hospitality in a language which by definition is not his own, the one imposed on him by the master of the house, the host, the king, the lord, the authorities, the nation, the State, the father, etc. This personage imposes on him translation into their own language, and that's the first act of violence.
>
> (2000, 15)

I arrived in the UK in the year 2000. I was not forced by political or economic reasons, but arrived with curiosity born from the desire to discover and understand a language that was not my own. I was drawn to the musicality of the unknown language, unable to understand at times, I initially relished the pleasure of not knowing. Then, methodically, I recorded the words that I was learning, in the moment, in a small notebook. I was learning through what Maurice Merleau-Ponty calls a process of sedimentation. I would absorb acquired meanings in specific situations and, in turn, I would try and use those words myself and constitute a prosody of my own. This was my right, I was in a European country, with free movement and free speech. No one had forced me to speak this foreign language, I had entered this foreign language of my own free will.

But today, or tomorrow, if I wished to remain whilst retaining my freedom of movement, something that only full citizenship would allow me, I would be *forced* to learn the language. Take an exam, obtain a certain result. The pleasure to learn, curiosity would turn into necessity. Can one take any pleasure in accomplishing a necessity, a duty? Perhaps. And yet the freedom to choose will be removed; my relationship to the English language will be altered.

> Autrement dit, il y aurait *antinomie*, une antinomie insoluble, une antinomie non dialectisable entre, d'une part, *La* loi de l'hospitalité, la loi inconditionnelle de l'hospitalité illimitée [...] et d'autre part, les lois de l'hospitalité, ces droits et ces devoirs toujours conditionnés et conditionnels [...].
>
> (Derrida 1997, 73)

In other words, there would be an antinomy, and insoluble antinomy, a non-dialectizable antinomy between, on the one hand, *The* law of unlimited hospitality [...], and on the other hand, the laws of (in the plural), those rights and duties that are always conditioned and conditional [...]

(Derrida 2000, 77)

The right to stay, *Indefinite Leave to Remain* is replaced today by *Settled Status* intended to European Citizens seeking the right of permanent residence. Both require the applicant to justify of five years of continuous residency in the country. Being a European citizen is no longer sufficient. A right acquired from birth has been removed and I am now subjected to the conditional rights described by Derrida. By the same account, I have been depleted of a sense of legitimacy.

The terminology itself, 'Leave to Remain,' leads to confusion. Is this deliberate? Can one think of a more striking opposition than this one? 'Leave' is a permission granted, the liberty to do something, as in 'Leave of Absence,' which means to give one permission to go on holidays. While the right to remain is granted, the right to move freely isn't; any prolonged absence of more than five consecutive years from the country will cost the right of residence. Right to remain admittedly, but accompanied by a conditional freedom of movement. The foreign body may no longer move freely and must comply with new sedentary rules. Will the *Settled Status* mark the end of the nomadic subject?

In the chapter titled "Propagation des ondes linguistiques" translated into "Propagation of linguistic waves" by Harris (1983), Saussure talks about the *sédentarisation* or settling down of linguistic communities through what he calls *'l'esprit de clocher.'* For Saussure, the *esprit de clocher* is the attachment to linguistic traditions learnt during childhood and repeated indefinitely amongst the same community. Wade Baskins (1959) translated the phrase into English using two words: 'individualism' and 'provincialism,' adding in square brackets the original *'esprit de clocher,'* whilst Roy Harris uses the work 'parochialism,' which also lacks the more architectural and geographical locus of a church spire (un *clocher*). According to Saussure, the indefinite repetition of linguistic traditions within the same community eventually leads to the dissolution of language into an infinite number of particularities. But he adds that the force of *esprit de clocher* is counteracted by a force of 'intercourse,' forcing individuals to interact and communicate.

The use of the word 'intercourse,' cited in English by Saussure himself, may raise a few eyebrows, but it is intended here in the sense of exchange and communication without any sexual connotation; there is no explicit reference to sex in Saussure's course. The word, however, cannot be ignored as it appears in a title and is somehow justified in a note by the editors, indicating that they thought it appropriate to "retain this picturesque expression, despite the fact that it was borrowed from the English language" (1916, 281). Saussure, it seems, has interleaved the English word knowingly and purposefully in order to illustrate and strengthen his argument for a free movement of language. On reading or hearing the word 'intercourse' in Saussure's course, the French speaker is surprised and will most definitely pause to question its relevance to the discussion on the propagation of languages. Did Saussure intend there to be a sexual dimension as well as a discursive one? Without any explicit description the reader is forced to draw his own conclusions. Saussure explains however that, contrary to received opinion, intercourse participates to the coherence of a language, and does so through a double phenomenon of resistance and validation of new words and innovations imported into a language:

> Si l'esprit de clocher rend les hommes sédentaires, l'intercourse les oblige à communiquer entre eux. C'est lui qui amène dans un village les passants d'autres localités, qui déplace une partie de la population à l'occasion d'une fête ou d'une foire, qui réunit sous les drapeaux les hommes de provinces diverses, etc. En un mot, c'est un principe unifiant, qui contrarie l'action dissolvante de l'esprit de clocher.
>
> (1916, 281–282)

> If parochialism makes men keep to themselves, intercourse forces them to communicate with others. Intercourse brings a village visitors from elsewhere, brings together people from all around on the occasion of a celebration or a fair, unites men from different provinces under the same flag. In short, intercourse is a principle of unification, which counteracts the disuniting influence of parochialism.
>
> (1983, 244)

Saussure himself was a true polyglot. He set off to establish linguistics as a new science precisely because of his great knowledge of numerous other languages, and the use of the English word here most aptly supports his main claim in this chapter: the necessity to go towards the language of the other, to intermingle to transform, to translate, to cross-pollinate for the sake of 'cohesion and extension' of language. It is up to the linguistic community however to accept or refute new words – and it should be noted that the word 'intercourse,' to this date, does not appear to be part of the French language. The word 'intercourse' introduced by Saussure during his *cours* deftly illustrates the principle of resistance, whereby the linguistic community refutes the word as 'picturesque' and clearly belonging to another language, thus reinforcing the cohesion of the French language.

In *Thresholds: A Prosody of Citizenship*, Robertson explains that we constitute ourselves as citizens according to the movement of subjectivity in language. But when translating the quote into French for this intervention I wondered whether I should use the word *langue, langage* or indeed *les langues*?[2] Robertson in fact talks about a totally different language to Saussure's *langue* as seen earlier, for her vernacular language can be multilingual:

> Characterized [...] by wit, excess, plasticity, admixture, surge, caesura, the wildness of a newly turned metaphor, polylinguality and inappropriateness, the vernacular is the name for the native complexity of each beginner as she quickens.
>
> (2018, 17)

Vernacular language is fluid, and just as there is no threshold to cross between *Domus* and *Civic*, but only a difference of scale, there is no threshold to cross between languages, for example, an institutionalised language, a literary language as understood by Saussure, or another. Two languages or more can be part of the same speaking subject as we have seen in Chapter 5 with Caroline Bergvall's multilingual poetry. Saussure explains that, often, languages are superimposed geographically as a result of displacements of population, whether by choice or through coercion. In his analysis of the 'Complications of geographic diversity,' he lists a number of causes of geographical superimpositions of languages, including invasions, colonisation and nomadic tribes bringing their languages [*leur parler*] with them. As a European nomadic subject[3] who had arrived in the UK by choice, I had brought with me the French language, *la langue française*. I had developed a personal prosody in French, and yet, upon arriving in the UK I became more preoccupied by the acquisition of the 'other' language, the language of the other. Edouard Glissant explained in an interview for *Le Monde* (2011) that he wrote "in the presence of all other languages of the world," and although I was certainly writing in the presence of the French language upon my arrival in the UK, this presence was a necessarily silent one, so as to be able to welcome the new language, the language of the other. Conversely, Derrida, in his seminar on hospitality, sees the mother tongue not as something which gives way to the new language, but as a force of resistance to the phenomenon of dislocation:

> Et bien la parole, la langue maternelle n'est pas seulement le chez-soi qui résiste, l'ipséité du soi qu'on oppose comme une force de résistance, comme une contre-force à ces dis-locations. La langue résiste à toutes les mobilités *parce qu*'elle se déplace avec moi. Elle est la chose la moins amovible, le corps propre le plus mobile qui reste la condition stable, mais portable, de toutes les mobilités [...].
> (1997, 83–85)

> Well, speech, the mother tongue, isn't only the home that resists, the ipseity of the self set up as a force of resistance, as a counter-force against these dis-locations. Language resists all mobilities *because* it moves about with me. It is the least immovable thing, the most mobile of personal bodies, which remains the stable but portable condition of all mobilities [...].
> (2000, 91)

Yet the French language itself, my mother tongue, evaded me while I was writing this paper, it resisted almost as much as the English language resisted when I first started writing in English. Every act of writing is as much an act of resistance as an act of *naissance* [birth].

For Derrida the mother tongue is a second skin one carries with oneself, but what then of the other language? The language of the other which has become the new language of the self? Has this new language become a second or third skin? If I agree with the non-detachable or non-removable quality of language, then I might not conceive of it as a second skin, but rather, to use Merleau-Ponty's words which I discussed in Chapter 5, the second language becomes a 'possible modulation' of my own body as expression (2012, 186). The second language is not a second skin but is part of my bodily system [appareil corporel] (1974, 19) and can be 'activated' as a mode of expression:

Et le sens de la parole n'est rien d'autre que la façon dont elle manie ce monde linguistique ou dont elle module sur ce clavier de significations acquises. Je le saisis dans un acte indivis, aussi bref qu'un cri.

(1945, 227)

And the sense of the speech is nothing other than the manner in which it handles this linguistic world, or in which it modulates upon this keyboard of acquired significations. I grasp it in an undivided act that is as brief as a cry.

(2012, 192)

We will note here that Merleau-Ponty's *parole*, translated as 'speech' by Landes, brings us a little closer to Robertson's 'prosody' of the speaking subject. This *parole*, or 'prosody,' might be considered as a modulation of different institutionalised or literary languages (if we were to use Saussure's terminology), yet all these languages are to be found in one and the same body; both languages in the case of the bilingual subject are indeed played in the same body, on the same 'keyboard of significations' that Merleau-Ponty refers to in the citation above. A little later in *Phénoménologie de la perception*, Merleau-Ponty claims that one can only live in one language at a time and does not have access to the '*full* sense' of several languages (1945, 228).[4] I would argue, however, that for the bilingual subject, the syntax and sonorities of the words encountered in different languages, in different situations, often in different countries and through various encounters, all become part of the speaking body's linguistic world. Both languages become available to the bilingual body at any given moment and are available as possible modulations of the same body, of the same speaking subject.

However, the desire of the bilingual speaking body to converge – or mobilise itself – towards a particular language, aside from the desire to communicate with the other, will also depend on her/his relationship to this particular language.

Following the Brexit vote in 2016, millions of European citizens living in the UK might see their rights of free movement removed and their relationship to the English language significantly altered as a result. The freedom of movement in Europe had created an environment where Robertson's idea of linguistic citizenship flourished, unbounded by any administrative border. Yet recent events mean that this situation is at risk and the *linguistic subjectivity* of European citizens living in the UK, and symmetrically, of UK citizens living in Europe, could be altered, whereby the learning of the 'other' language might become a necessary step in regaining the freedom of movement. The movement towards one or the other language might become for some a compulsory step in the application process to (re)gain the right of free movement.

Notes

1 A French version of this essay was presented on 10 July 2019 at the 23rd International Symposium for Phenomenology, organised by Emmanuel Alloa, Shela Sheikh and Delia Popa in Perugia, on the theme "L'Epreuve de l'Etranger: Translation, Migration, Resistance." Essay translated into English by the author.
2 For the translation of Saussure's terms *langue* and *langage*, see Chapter 1 of this volume.
3 Term developed by Rosi Braidotti in *Nomadic Subjects* (Columbia University Press, 2011).
4 Maurice Merleau-Ponty does not expand much on multilingualism but makes this remark in *Phénoménologie de la perception*:

> La prédominance des voyelles dans une langue, des consonnes dans une autre, les systèmes de construction et de syntaxe ne représenteraient pas autant de conventions arbitraires pour exprimer la même pensée, mais plusieurs manières pour le corps humain de célébrer le monde et finalement de le vivre. De là viendrait que le sens *plein* d'une langue n'est jamais traduisible dans une autre. Nous pouvons parler plusieurs langues, mais l'une d'elles reste toujours celle dans laquelle nous vivons. Pour assimiler complètement une langue, il faudrait assumer le monde qu'elle exprime et l'on n'appartient jamais à deux mondes à la fois.
>
> (1945, 228)

> The predominance of vowels in one language, of consonants in another, or systems of construction and syntax would not represent so many arbitrary conventions for expressing the same thought, but rather several ways for the human body to celebrate the world and to finally live it. This why the *full* sense of a language is never translatable into another. We can speak several languages, but one of them always remains the one in which we live. In order to wholly assimilate a language, it would be necessary to take up the world it expresses, and we never belong to two worlds at the same time.
>
> (2012, 193)

Works Cited

Derrida, Jacques. 1997. *De l'Hospitalité / Anne Dufourmantelle invite Jacques Derrida à répondre*. Paris: Calmann-Lévy.
———. 2000. *Of Hospitality / Anne Dufourmantelle invites Jacques Derrida to respond*, translated by Rachel Bowlby. California: Stanford University Press.

Glissant, Edouard. 2011. "Edouard Glissant: 'La langue qu'on écrit fréquente toutes les autres' " in *Le Monde*, 3 February.
Merleau-Ponty, Maurice. 1945. *Phénoménologie de la perception*. Paris: Gallimard.
———. 1974. *The Prose of the World*, translated by John O'Neill. London: Heinemann Educational Books.
———. 2012. *Phenomenology of Perception*, translated by Donald A. Landes. Oxon: Routledge.
Roberston, Lisa. 2012. *Nilling: Prose Essays on Noise, Pornography, the Codex, Melancholy, Lucretius, Folds, Cities and Related Aporias*. Toronto: Bookthug.
———. 2018. *Thresholds: A Prosody of Citizenship*. London: Book Works and The Common Guild.
Saussure, Ferdinand de. 1916. *Cours de linguistique générale*. Paris: Editions Payot & Rivages.
———. 1983. *Course in General Linguistics*, translated by Roy Harris. London: Bloomsbury
———. 1959. *Course in General Linguistics*, translated by Wade Baskin. New York: Columbia University Press.

Index

Note: *Italic* page numbers refer to figures and page numbers followed by "n" denote endnotes.

absolute movement 1, 6, 48, 51
academic conferences 5
Alice's Adventures in Wonderland 60
Alloa, Emmanuel 8
American Comparative Literature Association (ACLA) annual conference 79n1
appareil corporel 88
"Art in Translation" conference 7
Auster, Paul 28, 77

Bachelard, Gaston 38
Bailly, Charles 19n1
Barthes, Roland 12
Baskins, Wade 85
Benveniste, Emile 82, 83
Bergvall, Caroline 4, 7, 55–66
Berthoz, Alain 15, 16, 22, *23*, 24, 27, 46
bilingual 3, 7, 8, 59; bilingualism 3, 7, 21
bilingual body 8, 81–90
bilingual dictionaries 70
bilingual phenomenon 21, 32
bilingual space/bilingual vector field 32
bilingual subject 3, 17, 28, 34, 57, 60, 89
bodily sensations 46, 65, 71, 74
body 1–3, 6–8, 13, 14, 16–18, 22–25, 27, 33, 34, 37–39, 46–48, 57, 58, 61–66, 68–79, 81–90
The Brain's Sense of Movement (2000) 16
Butor, Michel 4, 6, 36–53

Calle-Gruber, Mireille 4
Carroll, Lewis 60
"Cat in the Throat" 57, 59
cavité buccale 13
City of Glass 28
Cixous, Hélène 3, 4, 56
co-citizens 83
communication 5, 8n1
Cornell, Sarah 56
Le corps comme expression et la parole 2, 3
'correlative movement' 26
Cours de linguistique générale (1916) 4, 10–19, 76; diagram *14*
Course in General Linguistics (1983) 5, 10
Critique du roman (1970) 37
"Crop" (2011) 7, 61
Cusset, François 70

Dallenbach, Lucien 44
dead language 75
degree zero 38
de Montaigne, Michel 3
depth 42, 44–45
Derrida, Jacques 3, 5, 16, 17, 34, 55, 56, 77, 81, 83, 88
Descartes, René 38, 45, *45*
"La différance" 16, 17
differentiation, principle 6
"Difficult Joys" 4
disambiguation 16
displacement, relative movement 39
distance 5, 24, 27, 36, 37, 39–52
Dürer, Albert 41

Index

The Ear of the Other (1985) 5
effort 2–3, 6, 24, 27, 33, 45, 51, 60–61, 66, 72, 77–79
effort of projection 46–47, 50, 51
effort of translation 51, 60
egocentric referential 22
Embodied Bilingualism 21
L'emploi du temps 40
English language 18, 70, 75, 81, 84, 86, 89
L'espace du roman (1964) 6, 39, 46
essays 3–4
Euclidean geometry 20, 21, 24
Evans, Robin 1, 6, 20, 21, 34
excess 56, 71, 73, 74, 87

folie 3, 7
foreign languages 68, 69
Forty, Adrian 18, 60
Foucault, Michel 82
French language 18, 77, 79, 81, 88

Le génie du lieu 36
geometrical transformations 6
geometrical translation 20–35
geometry 1, 6, 20–35, 38
Glissant, Edouard 87–88

Harris, Roy 5, 10–13, 85
Hatter, Mad 60
Heath, Stephen 12, 13
homophonic translation 68
hospitality 8, 83, 84, 88
Husserl, Edmund 6, 32–34, 38

Image, Music, Text 12
Improvisations 4
Intentionality and Intersubjectivity: A Phenomenological Study of Butor's La Modification 38, 48
intercourse, Saussure 87
interlingual translation 29
International Language Symposium, Dublin 5
international symposia 5
International Symposium for Phenomenology 8
investissement libidinal 76

Jakobson, Roman 29
Jespersen, Otto 13

Kamuf, Peggy 16
Koffka, Kurt 49

Lacan, Jacques 58
Lalangue 58
Landes, Donald A. 5, 15
language 1, 2, 3, 7, 10, 12, 17, 27, 55, 58, 82, 88–90
"Language, Migration and Diaspora" International Language Symposium 5, 35n1
langue 5, 33, 56, 58, 60, 61, 65, 82, 87; translating 10–19
les langues 55–66
Lawrence, T.E. 3
Leavy, John P. 34
Lecercle, Jean-Jacques 7, 56
Le Clézio, J.M.G. 74, 75
Lehrbuch der Phonetik (1904) 13
linguistic gymnastics 73
linguistic subjectivity 89
linguistic transformations 6
linguistic translation 1
linguistic weapon 69
literary language 3

madness 3, 78
Matthieussent, Brice 13
Merleau-Ponty, Maurice 1–6, 10–19, 27, 36–38, 40, 44, 45, 48, 49, 51, 56, 58–60, 63, 64, 66, 84, 88, 89
Meschonnic, Henri 82
mobile 46, 88
La modification (1957) 6; phenomenological reading of 36–53; second-person plural pronoun in 38; train journey for 47
Le Monolinguisme de l'autre 77
mother tongue 57, 58, 62, 68, 69, 76, 77, 81, 88
motricity 45; motor 24, 46
multilingual 7, 8, 59, 70, 87
multilingualism 7, 90n4
muscular effort 3, 24, 27, 39, 46–48

The New York Trilogy (1990) 28
Nilling (2012) 82
nonsense 7, 60, 61, 78, 79
Nouveau Roman 42, 44, 46

objectivism 14
Œuvres complètes 4
Oppenheim, Lois 38, 48
L'Oreille de l'autre (1982) 17
"The Origin of Geometry" (1989) 6, 32, 34
other, otherness 75, 77
'Otherness of Language' 77

paper, *communication* 5
'parapluie' 29
'parasol' 31, 32
parochialism 85, 86
parole 12, 58, 89
parole vive 4
Passage de Milan 40
Phénoménologie de la perception (Phenomenology of Perception) 2, 5, 6, 10–19, 45, 48, 51, 58, 63
phenomenology 6, 14, 15, 27, 36–53, 60
Philosophy of Nonsense (Lecercle) 55–66
poetical euphoria 58
Poincaré, Henri 6, 21, 22, 24, 26, 27, 46, 51
point kilomètrique zéro 39
political bilingual body 81–90
Popa, Delia 8
pre-linguistic state 7
"Propagation of linguistic waves" 85
La prose du monde 2, 59
Prosody of Citizenship 7, 82
provincialism 85

Le récit spéculaire 44
reformed body 68–79
reformed orthography 78
relative movement 51
representative space 24
Riedlinger, Albert 19n1
Riquet, Johannes 6, 53n1
Robertson, Lisa 7, 81–83, 87
running man drawing *23*

Saussure, Ferdinand de 4–6, 10–19, 28, 76, 79n2, 82, 85–87
Saussurean linguistics 69
"Say Parsley" (2010) 59
Le Schizo et les langues ou La Phonétique chez le psychotique: Esquisses d'un étudiant de langues schizophrénique (1970) 7
Science and Hypothesis (1902) 21
Séchehaye, Albert 19n1
second language 7, 88
sédentarisation 85
sedimentation 2, 84
self-translation 8
Sellers, Susan 56
sens (sense) 1–3, 5–7, 15, 18, 20–35, 55–66, 77, 78; translating 10–19, 33
Le sens du mouvement (1997) 15, 22, *23*, 46
sense of translation 6, 33, 34
sense of movement 8, 37, 46
"Le sens perdu (ou le 'Schizo' et la signification)" 75
Sheikh, Shela 8
"Signature, événement, context" (1972) 5, 8n1
signification 15
Smith, Colin 15
Société Nationale des Chemins de Fer Français (SNCF) 36
"The Spatiality of One's own Body and Motricity" 45
Spatial Modernities: Geography, Narratives, Imaginaries 6, 53n1
spatial translation 1
subjectivism 14

Three Steps on the Ladder of Writing (1993) 4, 55, 56
Thresholds: A Prosody of Citizenship 87
tongue (body part) 13, 14, 64
tongue (mother tongue) 57, 58, 62, 68, 69, 76, 77, 81, 88
"La Tour de Babil" 74
traducere 20
traduction 35
train carriage, expanding space 36–53

train itinerary 37
transitory 18
translating 10, 87; *langue* and *sens* 10–19
"Translation: Exchange of Ideas" 5
"Translation from Drawings to Buildings" 1, 20, 34
translation practice 13
"Translations: Exchange of Ideas" Conference 35n1
translators' notes 10–19
translatory phenomenon 27
"Travelling Narratives: Modernity and the Spatial Imaginary" Symposium 53n1

"Untitled Essay" 82

Van Rossum-Guyon, Françoise 37, 40
Vengeance du traducteur (2009) 13
vernacular language 82, 87
vestibular organ 23; canals *23*
The Violence of Language (1990) 56
"Le voyage et l'écriture" (1974) 36

Wolfson, Louis 7, 68–79
"Wolfson & Sons" 70
Words and Buildings: A Vocabulary of Modern Architecture (2000) 18